Landscape of the Body

Plays by John Guare

Bosoms and Neglect

Chaucer in Rome

Cop Out

A Few Stout Individuals

Four Baboons Adoring the Sun

General of Hot Desire

His Girl Friday (adaptation)

Home Fires

House of Blue Leaves

Lake Hollywood

Landscape of the Body

Lydie Breeze:
Part One: Women and Water
Part Two: Bulfinch's Mythology
Part Three: The Sacredness of the Next Task

Marco Polo Sings a Solo

Moon Under Miami

Muzeeka

Rich and Famous

Six Degrees of Separation

JOHN GUARE

Landscape of the Body

Grove Press
New York

FIRST EDITION

Library of Congress Cataloging-in-Publication-Data

Guare, John.
  Landscape of the body / by John Guare.
    p. cm.
  ISBN-10: 0-8021-4298-2
  ISBN-13: 978-0-8021-4298-6
  I. Title.
  PS3557.U2L3   2007
812'.54--dc22   2006048770

Grove Press
an imprint of Grove/Atlantic, Inc.
841 Broadway
New York, NY 10003

Distributed by Publishers Group West

www.groveatlantic.com

1   2   3   4   5   6   7   8   9   10   12   11   10   09   08   07

For Adele in 1977
The best part
For Adele still in 2007

WHAT IT WAS LIKE

Do you rewrite a play when it's revived?

First, a little history. I wrote *Landscape of the Body* in 1977. In 2004, Michael Greif did a terrific production of the play at the Williamstown Theater Festival under the aegis of Michael Ritchie, with Lili Taylor and Sherie Rene Scott as the two sisters. Michael Greif wanted to underline the musical elements of the play in a way that had never been done before. He hired the young composer J. Michael Friedman to take the songs I had written for the play and use them as the basis for a score to be played by an omnipresent four-piece jazz combo that would roll in and out on Allen Moyer's set and play throughout the entire show, making it a true melodrama. That musical decision expanded the part of Rosalie—not by words but by her presence in every scene. I loved the mad comic energy Sherie Rene brought to the part, which in turn intensified the depth of Lili Taylor's brutally honest performance. We had had a terrific time working on the play during our two-week run in the Berkshires. Then a year later James Houghton called.

James Houghton is the estimable founder of the Signature Theatre on West Forty-second Street in New York City, which has an extraordinary mission. Every year, the Signature devotes one season to the work of one playwright. Edward Albee, Arthur Miller, Sam Shepard, Adrienne Kennedy have been some of the previous playwrights so honored. August Wilson would be the subject of the 2005–2006 season. August, unaware at this time of the illness that would prove fatal, asked James if he could delay his scheduled season to 2006–2007, as he was finishing *Radio Golf,* which would be the last play in his epic ten-play cycle. James agreed and asked Horton Foote and me, previous Signature playwrights, if we could fill out the suddenly blank season with Horton's *The Trip to Bountiful* and my *Landscape of the Body*.

Absolutely.

I was eager for a chance to get back to work with this cast on the play. Miraculously, Lili was available in the spring of 2006. Sherie Rene could get a leave from her Broadway musical. Would I change anything? Let me think about that.

Michael Greif and the brilliant cast we had assembled asked me why I had written the play in 1977 in the first place.

That was easy to answer. Happiness. I had met the woman who'd become my wife on Nantucket in 1975 and it looked as if Adele and I might actually work out, or, more to the point, that I might not mess it up. I was finally living in my future. I searched out a play to mark this time.

One day while walking along Hudson Street in Greenwich Village, where I lived (I was probably mumbling a song to myself —I don't know—"New York, New York! A helluva town, the Bronx is—"), a flash of yellow crashed into me. A spandex-clad cyclist leaned over my body, sprawled on the pavement, and yelled down at me, "You broke the chain on my ten-speed Raleigh! You broke the chain on my ten-speed Raleigh bike! I wish you were dead! Die! Die! Are you dead?" He went off, pushing his lopsided yellow racer, screaming, "Die! Die!" I limped home. Nothing broken, but suppose I had died? Worse—suppose something happened to Adele? What would happen if I lost all this? How permanent was this unusual, precious happiness that she had brought to my life? What was the shelf life of our time together? I suddenly could imagine dying. The unimaginable became imaginable. But if I lost everything, what would I be left with? What if something happened to— No, I couldn't even think it. Everything seemed to be so perilous, life merely waiting to be broken by a yellow spandex flash out of nowhere. Is it all Mary Tyrone's last line in O'Neill's *Long Day's Journey into Night:* "And then I . . . was so happy for a time"?

I had to remind Michael Greif and the cast that things in the seventies were not so hot for little old New York. Like me and that cyclist, the city constantly careened on the brink of collapse. Basic services vanished. Garbage seemed to collect everywhere on the streets. Gangs of thugs would set those piles of trash on fire. Lots of street crime. People exchanging mugging stories became the new small talk. "I gave him all I had. He waved his gun at me: 'Is this it?' 'Would you take a check?'" Graffiti tattooed walls, windows, buses, billboards, parks. An English friend said the graffiti made each subway train zoom into the station with the force of an obscene phone call. On October 30, 1975, the New York *Daily News* headline immortalized President Gerald Ford's response to this blight: FORD TO CITY: DROP DEAD.

I also had to point out to this young cast what was going on in the Village in those days. A massive, oppressive construction called the West Side Highway ran above and along the abandoned rotting piers that lined the Hudson River on West Street from Christopher Street to Fourteenth Street. In the round-the-clock darkness under the highway trucks were parked, block after block of trucks, their rear doors hanging open, inviting anyone who desired to climb in, turning this underbelly into an ulcerous parking lot from hell. A sub-subculture of illicit sex, drugs, violence festered in the backs of these trucks. Were they abandoned? Where did they come from? You would never walk along the river at night unless you were feeling suicidal.

Don't forget the unsolved Greenwich Village "bag murders"; butchered bodies in black plastic bags would float in the Hudson right off this hellhole. And just to keep you on your toes: a gang of wild neighborhood kids went around beating up people at random.

Yet I was the happiest I'd ever been in my life.

"We'll have Manhattan / the Bronx and Staten / Island too."

When I met Adele in 1975, I was living in the Village near the river on Bank Street in what had been John Lennon's apartment before he moved uptown to meet his fate in the Dakota. What an apartment! It consisted of two rooms, the first being the ground-floor length of the brownstone building, windowless and very dark; the second room was all light, a thirty-foot ceiling, banks of skylights, a spiral staircase leading to a roof garden. An unnamed sculptor decades before had built this dream studio on what had been the brownstone's garden.

Part of me loved living in the shabby residue of John Lennon's fame. It made me interesting. Another part of me refused to face the fact that the apartment was unlivable. The studio room with the thirty-foot ceilings and skylights was impossible to heat in the winter. The drinks by my bed would freeze during a January night. In the summer it would take a nuclear-powered A/C to tame this thirty-foot-high inferno.

I asked the landlord, "Why did John Lennon move out?" "He wanted more room." And I said, "But that's why I'm moving in." The rent for the time was outrageous. Five hundred dollars a month. I took it.

All that remained of John and Yoko was a large bed in the center of the room with a number of posts around it; attached to each post was a television set tuned to one channel; in pre-cable days this meant seven TVs, seven stations. My predecessors apparently would stay in bed wearing headsets whose sound channels they would switch as they switched (or didn't switch) their eyes. A large closet contained a secret room in the cellar. You could find the trapdoor only by lifting the carpet in the closet floor. I went down there once. No, this airless tomb was a remnant of the Inquisition. I never made the descent again.

The first night I moved in I heard scratching at the front door, which led up a short flight of stairs onto the street. "John?" the voice said. "Who is it?" I asked brightly as I started to unlock the door, sure it was some pal stopping by to see my new glamour pad. The desperate voice mewled, "John, let me in. I've come such a long way." Which friend was playing a joke? "No, who is it?" "John, let me in. I love you." "Tell me who you are?" "John, I love you. Let me in." The creepy urgency in the late-night voice was no joke. I didn't open the door. The scratching and weeping continued all night. I opened the door in the morning. Bouquets of wilted flowers lined the doorstep with a card: "I love you John."

Almost every day in the four years I lived there I would find sprays of roses or chrysanthemums left at the door or elaborately decorated cakes with "John Forever" in frosting or long, yearning confessional letters that only John—the other John, the real John—would understand. They told me their secrets.

In those pre-Internet days, these pilgrims had not yet learned that the object of their obsession had moved uptown; 105¼ Bank Street (yes, ¼; not ½) was still the requisite destination for their hajj. I'd say to the anguished spiritual travelers huddling outside my door, "He doesn't live here." "But we've come so far. Australia. Japan. New Zealand. Oregon. Germany. Where is he?" Sometimes they'd get very angry. "Hey, don't get mad at me. I'm not hiding him. He doesn't live here. I swear to you. Yoko doesn't live here. No, I don't know where he went. Back off." "Let us in." "No, you can't come in." "We want peace!" "I want peace!" "We *have* to come in!"

I understood that. I wanted "in" somewhere as well. I wanted peace as well. What was my life going to be? I inadvertently lived in a world that for so many others was the Mecca of desperate dreams. Why couldn't I be that John? Once, someone left a delicately painted, self-proclaimed official passport ensuring John free passage to anywhere in the universe. Why couldn't I have a passport like that to get me out of that place Wallace Stevens described so accurately where one's desire is too difficult to tell from despair.

I had a baby grand piano I loved to play, gleefully torturing my next-door neighbors John Cage and Merce Cunningham, who would pound on the wall for me to shut up. Across the street was the HB Studio, founded by Uta Hagen, the legendary actress who was the original and greatest Martha in Edward Albee's *Who's Afraid of Virginia Woolf?,* and her husband, Herbert Berghof, no slouch of an actor himself. Men and women and children of all ages took acting classes at the Hagen/Berghof Studio on what seemed to be a twenty-four-hour schedule. Some days you'd see the great Uta herself striding up Bank Street followed by a group of her acolytes receiving life transfusions from her aura, shouldering the weight of their dreams as they followed her to and from class. You could hear the students talking earnestly in the street. The conversation seemed to consist of a chant: Uta says. Uta said. Uta told me. Uta Uta Uta.

And then there was upstairs in my building. I learned never to live in the same building with the furtive love interest of a Major American Drama Critic. MADC was having a hot romance with a woman who lived upstairs at 105 Bank. I vaguely knew MADC and his wife, making him Married MADC. I did not want to become an eyewitness to the MMADC's clandestine life while MMADC could still be reviewing any of my plays. Would he make me pay for knowing his secret? I'd just stay out of the way. Don't let him know I know. I'd leave my apartment, size up today's crowd of Lennonites, make sure MMADC wasn't coming down or going up the front steps, and then I'd trot up the street to do my day's errands—and watch out for yellow bikes. When I wasn't writing, I liked to (and still do) walk around the Village. In 1973 I'd stop in at the Lilac Chocolate Shop on Christopher Street, drop in at the great Phoenix Bookstore on Jones Street and the Riviera for a drink, then some unnamed junk shop by Hudson that sold stacks of old *Life* magazines and comic books from my childhood—*Mandrake the Magician, Captain Marvel, The Shadow.* See what Godard or Truffaut or Altman was playing at the Eighth Street movie theater. Browse at Wilentz's Eighth Street bookshop. Once at two a.m. I went to the twenty-four-hour supermarket a block from Bank Street to get some coffee. A uniformed chauffeur pushed a cart down an aisle. Beside him a beautiful African-American woman in a sable coat tossed bread and milk and coffee into the cart. I couldn't believe it. I said, "Leontyne Price in D'Agostino's at two in the morning?" She said, "Honey, even a diva's got to eat."

Then in the midst of all this I met Adele and discovered another truth: "There lives the dearest freshness deep down things" (Gerard Manley Hopkins, "God's Grandeur").

Landscape of the Body came together out of incredible happiness and daily violence and insatiable yearning in this failing city that dreamed of success.

One morning after the cyclist incident, I said my good morning to the day's gaggle hoping for a sighting of their master, disappointed them, checked that MMADC wasn't fleeing down the front stairs of the brownstone hoping for the magical appearance of a cab to take him home, and went up to the coffee shop on the corner of Hudson Street for breakfast. As I ate my poached eggs I noticed two boys and two girls—fourteen, tops—who should have been in school, whispering in a booth. The boys were proud young roosters telling the girls the most fascinating tale anyone had ever heard. What caught my eye was this: the boys' arms were each lined with wristwatches, ten or eleven on each scrawny arm. The enthralled girls, leaning forward, flicked the straps of the gold watches. I tried to hear what the boys were saying but couldn't get close enough.

I went home and wrote down what I thought those kids were saying. That became the first scene I wrote for *Landscape of the Body*.

I'd been writing songs and wanted those songs in the play. That's the best part of making plays: the things you like to write determine the style of your play. I would need a singer to sing the songs; she would tell us the story. What was the story? Of course: She was killed by the cyclist who hit me but she kept on singing! Why should death stop her career?

Sometimes happiness gives you the security you need to go into the dark places.

Other people from my life showed up. Durwood Peach was the summertime Good Humor man when I was a kid out on Long Island. Durwood was from South or North Carolina and a very good-humored man indeed. I remembered Raulito, a young Cuban who worked on *Two Gentlemen of Verona* (a musical I wrote for the New York Shakespeare Festival with Galt MacDermot and Mel Shapiro] as Raul Julia's dresser. What would my Raulito do? Wait—I know! When I got out of the air force in 1964 I had worked for a travel agency on Fourteenth Street and Eighth Avenue whose main activity was working the phones, luring people down to our place of business by telling them they had won a holiday on the chance the boss could sell them a real vacation. Raulito would own the travel agency in the play.

But who was the central character?

And then Alice Crimmins in her red hair and heavy makeup and red slutty toreador pants stepped up to the plate. Alice Crimmins was a great-looking dame, described in her trial as a "former cocktail waitress," who wore lots of white makeup to cover teen acne scars. In the 1960s she was charged with murdering her two young children on the grounds they stood in the way of her social life, which meant in the press "affairs with numerous men."

I had actually seen the notorious Alice in the flesh! In the sixties, the Women's House of Detention occupied the weirdly shaped city block at West Tenth Street and Sixth Avenue. (Today the prison has new life as the Jefferson Market Library.) People lined up on Tenth Street around the clock to scream up into the turrets of the jail, trying to find an inmate, trying to have an intimate talk with a friend or relative who leaned out between bars five floors above the street. One day, I saw Alice Crimmins either getting out of the squad car to go into the jail or coming out of the jail to go to her trial. I loved reading about the sensational case. The papers reported her as saying, "They're prosecuting me for my lifestyle." Maybe she had a point. It was typical in these days with the injustice of Vietnam raging that society could go after somebody, hound her for being a waitress at a cheesy, semi-topless, faux–Playboy Club somewhere out in Queens. But here was Alice, who had lost everything— her kids, her livelihood, her freedom—and she was still defiant.

I had never said "I'm going to write a play about Alice Crimmins." She just showed up and the play took off. Only now she had a sister and her name was Betty and she was from Bangor, Maine. And she had a fourteen-year-old son, Bert.

I was in the homestretch of writing and had taken the phone off the hook in Mecca on Bank Street when the doorbell rang and rang. Some kid bringing yet another token of adoration to John Lennon? Ring ring. I ran to the door to stop the ringing. Bill Gardner stood there. Bill ran the Academy Festival Theater in Lake Forest, Illinois, where I had done a play in 1973. The legendary production of O'Neill's *Moon for the Misbegotten* with Jason Robards and Colleen Dewhurst started life at his theater. Irene Worth opened *Sweet Bird of Youth* there. Rip Torn and Geraldine Page did both *A Streetcar Named Desire* and *Little Foxes* there. Quite a summer theater. And Bill was a terrific guy to boot. He said, "I'm in town—your phone wasn't working—have I come at a bad time?" I said, "Come in, I'm finishing a play." I sat him down, gave him the first act of *Landscape,* and went back typing. He took the pages as I ripped them out of the typewriter.

I got to the end. If you lose everything, what remains? Rosalie the dead sister in the last scene of the play gives her sister Betty the worst advice I've ever heard—travel alone, don't trust anyone—advice that I had previously built my life on. I ended the play on the hint that Betty might finally stop listening to the world around her and take a new tack. Yes, there might just be something inexhaustible in the human spirit that constantly says *Yes* once more.

I finished the play. I wrote the title page. I wrote a page dedicating it to Adele. I was exhausted. I was thirsty. I put the phone back on the hook. Bill finished reading the play a few pages after I finished typing. He said, "I'll produce it." "When?" "It's May. Let's do it in July."

We went up to the copy shop and got it duplicated. I had seen Shirley Knight in Robert Patrick's *Kennedy's Children* on Broadway and wanted her for the lead. It turned out she lived a few blocks away. I got her the play that very day. She called back a few hours later. What were the dates? She'd do it. I had loved F. Murray Abraham in Terrence McNally's *The Ritz;* he said yes when I asked him to play Holahan. Peg Murray, who'd won a Tony for *Cabaret* and was a great musical performer, would play Rosalie, the dead singing sister. Richard Bauer, a maniacally funny actor from Washington's Arena Stage, would play Raulito. A remarkable musician named Wally Harper would supply the musical accompaniment.

Landscape of the Body opened in Lake Forest in July 1977. I don't read reviews but Adele made me read the part of Richard Christiansen's review in the *Chicago Tribune* that declared, "As 1975 was the year of *A Chorus Line,* so 1977 will be the year of *Landscape of the Body.*"

That sounded promising.

Joe Papp loved it and we opened in New York in October 1977 at the Public Theater. Thanks to *A Chorus Line,* Joe had the cash to give us an elaborate production. Was it too lavish a production? First of all, the set featured these two massive turntables. *Annie,* the big musical on Broadway, had one turntable. If I'm ever out of nightmares, I just summon up those two massive turntables, which were always breaking down or, better yet, groaning in their inexorable revolves. We ran our scheduled sixty-four performances. Was it the turntables?

A friend who saw both productions twenty-nine years apart said the big difference was in 1977 one spent two hours and fifteen minutes in this grim world and then left the theater and walked out into the exact same grimness. In 2006 the city had been transformed, reborn now for many years. When Rosalie told her adventure of making her porn movie back in 1977, she only had to say she went to a motel on Forty-second Street, way over west, to define the epitome of sleaze, the ultimate bottom of the barrel, the place where you went when you wanted to go as low as you could go. In 2006 that line got a terrific laugh. By then, Forty-second Street, way over west, was lined with a Starbucks, a health club, a supermarket up the street, shiny high-rise apartments down the street along the Hudson—and the Signature Theatre.

After *Landscape of the Body* closed at the end of 1977, I happily left Bank Street and all its dreams and dreamers and found a real life with Adele in another part of the Village, where we still live. But *Landscape of the Body* kept on as part of my life.

The Dramatists Guild awarded it the Hull-Warriner Prize as Best Play of the 1977–1978 season.

Sam Spiegel, the movie mogul who had made *On the Waterfront* and *Lawrence of Arabia,* bought the movie rights. He wanted to make a quick picture the way he had with Tennessee Williams's *Suddenly, Last Summer.* Yes! Remember Liz Taylor in that white bathing suit? I was thrilled. Sam said in his guttural basso, "First of all, you cannot have the dead singer telling the story. That belongs to the theater. You must cut Rosalie and the songs and tell the story unvarnished." I took his advice. So long, Rosalie.

I loved working with Sam in his Park Avenue penthouse under his Cézannes. I spent 1978 and into 1979 working on the screenplay with him. I also had written a new play called *Bosoms and Neglect* that was going to be done in Chicago at the Goodman Theater and might come to New York. Sam said, "If the new play is a success, I want you and Adele to come to Cannes and be my guests on my yacht for a Mediterranean cruise." I said, "Suppose it gets bad reviews?" Sam: "Then you cannot come." "Suppose it gets mixed reviews?" Sam: "Then you and Adele can come to the dock and watch us sail away."

The new play opened. We did not go on the cruise.

When I finally gave Sam my screenplay for *Landscape of the Body* he read it and sighed: "You've done everything I asked you to do. The only problem is if we make this movie, it will be so depressing the only place we can open it is Jonestown." I looked at the Cézannes for the last time and left.

The lesson was simple: Theater is essentially poetry. Film is essentially documentary, passively recording whatever data flow in front the camera. Is the enemy naturalism, which says if it looks authentic then it is authentic? For me, the very essence of theater is to reveal to the audience the invisible forces that shape and color and carbonate our lives. Write that on the blackboard a thousand times. Because I wanted to please Sam, I removed all that was theatrical from my play—all the songs, all the interplay between stage and audience. I cut the theatrical heart out of the play and delivered the ashen residue of a sordid little tale. How to make sure I keep my theater a place for poetry became my mantra. I began my war against the kitchen sink.

In the summer of 1979 the French film director Louis Malle called me and asked if I was the guy who had written the play about the mother suspected of killing her kid that he had seen at the Public Theater a year and a half before. Yes. He had money for a movie but nothing to shoot. Did I have any ideas? As a matter of fact I did. I took him to Atlantic City the next day. Working with Louis on the movie *Atlantic City* began one of the great friendships of my life.

People always lament what the city used to be, or what a neighborhood once was. That's what I love about New York City—it's always being reborn, it's always reinventing itself. And it demands the same of you—that you keep readjusting to time.

xviii

You can't live in the past in this city, you can't lament and say, "Oh, oh, oh." It's just not there anymore. New York forces you to do the most challenging thing: accept reality.

Over the years *Landscape of the Body* has had a number of terrific productions with splendid actors such as Christine Lahti and Laura Linney playing Betty. But none of the elements ever came together as they did at the Signature Theatre in April 2006. We opened. Adele burst into tears and said, "It's taken twenty-nine years to get it right."

So do you rewrite a play when it's revived?

I did make one change at the Signature. I moved the song that opened Act Two to the end of Act One, and that's where it always should have been.

But do you rewrite a play?

You can't. Every play is a landmark in a playwright's life, telling you where you were, who you were, what you were, for better or for worse, when you wrote the specific play. While writing this play I was incredibly happy. The happiness now is no less profound; it's just a different, deeper kind.

What is it like to revisit this play now? I'm not revisiting it. I never left it.

Landscape of the Body

Landscape of the Body was first produced by William Gardner at the Academy Festival Theater, in Lake Forest, Illinois, in July 1977. It was directed by John Pasquin; the settings were by John Wulp; costumes were by Laura Crow; and the lighting was by Jennifer Tipton. The stage mechanics were by Robert Giffen; the production pianists were Rod Derefinko and William Snyder; and the stage manager (in both Lake Forest and New York) was Steven McCorkle. The cast, in order of appearance, was as follows:

BETTY	Shirley Knight
CAPTAIN MARVIN HOLAHAN	F. Murray Abraham
ROSALIE	Peg Murray
RAULITO	Richard Bauer
BERT	Paul McCrane
DONNY	Anthony Marciona
JOANNE	Alexa Kenin
MARGIE	Bonnie Deroski
MASKED MAN	Jay Sanders
DURWOOD PEACH	Rex Robbins
DOPE KING OF PROVIDENCE	Jay Sanders
BANK TELLER	Jay Sanders

Landscape of the Body was then presented in New York City by Joseph Papp at the Public Theater (New York Shakespeare Festival) on October 12, 1977. It was directed by John Pasquin; the settings and costumes were by Santo Loquasto; lighting was by Jennifer Tipton; musical arrangements and incidental music were by Wally Harper; and the associate producer was Bernard Gersten. The pianist was Rod Derefinko. The cast, in order of appearance, was as follows:

BETTY	Shirley Knight
CAPTAIN MARVIN HOLAHAN	F. Murray Abraham
ROSALIE	Peg Murray
RAULITO	Richard Bauer
BERT	Paul McCrane
DONNY	Anthony Marciona
JOANNE	Alexa Kenin
MARGIE	Bonnie Deroski
MASKED MAN	Raymond J. Barry
DURWOOD PEACH	Remak Ramsay
DOPE KING OF PROVIDENCE	Raymond J. Barry
BANK TELLER	Raymond J. Barry

Landscape of the Body was again presented in New York City, on April 16, 2006, by the Signature Theatre Company (James Houghton, founding artistic director; Kathryn M. Lipuma, executive director) at the Peter Norton Space. It was directed by Michael Greif; musical direction and additional music, Michael Friedman; sets by Allen Moyer; costumes by Miranda Hoffman; lighting by Howell Binkley; sound by Brett R. Jarvis; fight direction, Rick Sordelet; dialect coach, Stephen Gabis; production stage manager, Cole Bonenberger; artistic associate, Beth Whitaker; production manager, Chris Moses. The cast, in order of appearance, was as follows:

BETTY	Lili Taylor
CAPTAIN MARVIN HOLAHAN	Paul Sparks
ROSALIE	Sherie Rene Scott
RAULITO	Bernard White
BERT	Stephen Scott Scarpulla
DONNY	Paul Iocono
JOANNE	Jill Shackner
MARGIE	Colby Minifie
MASKED MAN	Brian Sgambati
DURWOOD PEACH	Jonathan Fried
DOPE KING OF PROVIDENCE	Brian Sgambati
BANK TELLER	Brian Sgambati

THE PLAY TAKES PLACE ON A FERRY TO NANTUCKET
AND
IN GREENWICH VILLAGE.

ACT ONE

The deck of a ferry boat sailing from Hyannis to Nantucket.

A WOMAN sits writing notes on the deck. She is bundled up in layers of clothes against the cool. She has shopping bags around her feet. When she finishes one note, she rolls it into a cylinder and inserts it into a bottle she takes out of the shopping bags. She seals the bottle and tosses it overboard. She watches it go. She begins another.

A MAN is watching her. He is heavily disguised. Comic false eyeglasses and nose with mustache dangling beneath. Muffler wrapped high. Hat pulled down. He carries a little suitcase.

MAN   That's the Kennedy compound over there. I bought a postcard at the bus station in Hyannis and the postcard tells you whose house is who.

He proffers it. She looks at it briefly, looks at the shore, and resumes her note writing.

MAN   That house is Teddy Kennedy's and that house was where Jack lived and that house is where the parents lived and that house is where the sister Eunice lived and that house is where the sister Jean lived and that house— The postcard seems not to match up to reality. I get them all mixed up now, it's been so long. Empty rooms. Open windows. White curtains blowing out.

She looks up, tosses another bottle over, and watches it go.

MAN   I won a contest in grammar school knowing the names of the Dionne Quintuplets. I could rattle them off. Emilie. Annette. See. I can't even remember. Yvonne. And the worst is nobody remembers the Dionne Quintuplets. You tell young people, younger than we are, about the Dionne

I

Quintuplets and they don't know who you're talking about.

WOMAN Emilie was the left-handed one. Emilie was the only left-handed Dionne Quintuplet. What was the name of the doctor who delivered the Dionne Quintuplets?

MAN Dr. Dafoe.

WOMAN Dr. Dafoe.

MAN We could have a marriage made in heaven sharing information like that.

WOMAN I'm not in the market.

MAN I went down to Washington in 1960 for Kennedy's inauguration. They were selling at the Union Station an entire set of dishes of china and every plate was a different Kennedy. The big meat platter was Poppa Joe. The other cake platter had Momma Rose on it. John-John and Caroline were on little bread-and-butter plates. You're so open to talk to. Generally on trips of this nature—three-hour ferry trips from the mainland to an island—you begin talking to your fellow shipmates desperately leaping into conversational gambits, reduced to buying dusty postcards of abandoned compounds of families who once made all the difference in America. I begin talking and you pick right up on it. We could have a marriage made in heaven. We can talk. I think that's why marriages fail. People can't talk. People fight to have something to talk about. People kill each other, say, because the words don't come into place. I think of murder, say, as a sentence that did not make it through the computer up here in the head. If people had a better grasp of language, of syntax, of the right word, of being understood, you'd hear that crime rate, you'd see that homicide rate plunge like those bottles you're tossing over

. . . Would they be sentences you'd be writing on that piece of paper?

She tosses another bottle over.

MAN   What attracted you to me first? My confidence-inspiring voice? My ability to select the proper word out of the autumn air? A poll said what women notice most in men was their butts. Is that it? You liked my ass? Is that what attracted you to me? Are the polls right? My confidence is in bad disrepair and needs all the propping up it can beg, borrow, or infer.

WOMAN   I saw you getting on the boat. I wondered if you were in disguise. I said to myself, Is this a masquerade cruise? Then I thought, This is a man with a facial cancer and his face has been removed and replaced by a necessary false nose to disguise the two gaping holes under there. A false mustache to cover the missing upper lip. False eyebrows to cover the grafted skin around the eyeballs which still function or he'd be tapping a white cane around this deck. He walks with a steady stride. No, I won't have to be yelling Man Overboard. It's a disguise.

MAN   You recognized me?

WOMAN   Captain Marvin Holahan. Sixth Precinct Homicide.

The man pulls off his disguise.

HOLAHAN   What did you write in that note? A confession?

She throws sheets of small papers into the wind. They blow away.

BETTY   A confession. A full confession. I wrote down everything that happened. And it's all gone. There it goes! There's your case.

3

They face each other. The lights go down on them. They both take off their coats. She wears a tight sexy dress. The light is harsh in this interrogation room. She sits in a chair. He circles her. He shines a desk lamp in her eyes.

VOICE Flashback. Five months before. Marvin Holahan. Betty Yearn. Sixth Precinct. New York City. A spring day. Easter Sunday. Vernal equinoxes. The sun and moon cross each other's path.

BETTY I don't see how you can ask me these questions.

HOLAHAN Easy.

BETTY At this point in my life in history you could ask me these questions.

HOLAHAN The kid is dead.

BETTY I cannot cannot cannot—draw underlines under the cannot—cannot cannot cannot—six negatives make a positive—cannot understand—

HOLAHAN How I can ask you these questions?

BETTY How you can ask me these questions—

HOLAHAN Lady, I'm not talking simple child battering.

BETTY The kid is dead. The kid is dead. You leave out the fact it's my kid.

HOLAHAN Decapitation, Betty.

BETTY My son is dead. My boy is dead. My kid killed. Not the kid. My kid.

HOLAHAN The head chopped off, Betty. That's not Family Court. Chopped-off heads are not referrals to Family Counseling. That goes beyond battering.

4

BETTY   Not the kid. My kid. My kid.

HOLAHAN   You and your boyfriend didn't say my kid when you got out the hacksaw. You must've said, oh, let me guess: You little bastard.

BETTY   I'm not going to throw up.

HOLAHAN   What did your kid see, Betty, that you had to chop his head off?

BETTY   If I throw up, it's like you win. You're not going to win.

HOLAHAN   Where's the boy's father?

BETTY   I haven't seen him in years.

HOLAHAN   Maybe the boy's father did it in revenge against you?

BETTY   Strangers don't do revenge. The father didn't even know where we live. I feel like I'm standing in that corner over there watching me, and if I try hard enough I can switch the dial and I'll see me on another channel. I'd like a laugh track around my life. I'd like a funny theme introducing my life. I'm standing right over in that corner watching me.

HOLAHAN   Was your boy a homosexual?

BETTY   He's fourteen, for God's sake.

HOLAHAN   Lady, we got bodies coming in here don't even live to be fourteen. Their ages never get off the fingers of two hands.

BETTY   There's a whole series of homosexual murders going on down there at Christopher Street. Maybe the kid was into something. I don't think so. Don't those murders involve decap— The heads off . . .

5

HOLAHAN   How do you know about that?

BETTY   Is that the clue that gives myself away? I read the papers. I hear on the street. Did you follow up that clue? Why did you drag me in here? I'm supposed to be out there, mourning, weeping—

HOLAHAN   Betty, I'm trying to be kind. If you're embarrassed confessing to such a heinous crime, you want me to get Sergeant Lorraine Dean down here? There ain't nothing Lorraine hasn't heard. She's a good woman, a good listener, heavy in the ankles, platinum blonde, a nice soft bosom that I swear has got Seconal and Librium in. She'd hold you and rock you in the cradle of the deep and she'll sing "I'm confessing that I love you . . ." She'll sing that and make it easy for you to talk about what you did and get you help. She's got a nice voice, Lorraine does. She could've made it big in the show biz department were it not for her tragedy in the ankle department. Should I get Lorraine down here and you can tell her all? You want Lorraine? "I just found joy. I'm as happy as a baby boy. With another brand-new choo choo toy when I marry my Lorraine!" Betty? You could tell me too? There's nothing hasn't been poured into these ears. I'm taking courses at NYU nights in psychology. Things like you did happen all the time. We even had a spot quiz last week on a woman, went into a deep depression, drowned her two kids. Two! You just did one. Imagine how she feels. But they were infants. And she drowned them. I can't wait to ask my teacher about decapitation. You might help me get an honors. I might do a paper on you. Most infanticides are drownings or smotherings or an occasional throwing off a bridge . . .

BETTY I remember when I was little kid at the end of the McCarthy hearings when Joe McCarthy was destroying human lives, this great lawyer—

HOLAHAN Welch. Joseph Welch.

BETTY Stood up and said to McCarthy: Is there no such thing as human decency? And that question shocked everybody and destroyed Joe McCarthy.

HOLAHAN I'll tell you that great lawyer Welch after that made a film for Otto Preminger called *Anatomy of a Murder* starring James Stewart and Lee Remick. Is there no such thing as human decency left?

BETTY Is there no such thing as human decency left?

HOLAHAN A damn good little question.

BETTY Will I get off to go to my son's funeral?

HOLAHAN Is Otto Preminger filming it?

BETTY Am I booked? What's up? Do I go to my son's funeral?

HOLAHAN Did you kill him?

BETTY Do I get off for the funeral?

HOLAHAN Say yes, beautiful Betty, and there's no place you can't go.

BETTY I want my boy buried in Bangor, Maine, with his grandparents and his aunts and his uncles. I want him buried in Bangor with my father, with my sister Rosalie. Where I'll be buried when I die. I want him there. I want him out of New York.

7

HOLAHAN   You think it's fair to be at the funeral when you caused the funeral?

BETTY   I'm sorry, Your Honor, Mr. Kangaroo Court. I missed his death.

HOLAHAN   I keep thinking you were there.

BETTY   What is my motive? I cannot believe I am a suspect in my own son's death. I am supposed to be comforted. I am supposed to be held and allowed to cry and not made to feel . . . There's no insurance. I am no beneficiary. I cannot believe. I don't kill my own flesh and blood. I don't kill me. If I wanted to kill him, I would've killed me along with him. I don't kill me. I am here. Am I a car? A car you have to pull over to the side of the road and give a ticket to? You have to torture a certain number of people a day? Is this torture a routine formality? My boy is dead. I would like to grieve.

HOLAHAN   When did you come to New York?

BETTY   Two years ago.

HOLAHAN   Why?

BETTY   To get my sister.

HOLAHAN   Where is your sister now?

BETTY   My sister's dead.

HOLAHAN   Let me get this straight. You came to New York two years ago to get your dead sister.

BETTY   She was not dead at the time.

HOLAHAN   You came to New York two years ago alone to get your sister.

BETTY   Not alone. With Bert.

8

HOLAHAN   Bert? Bert?

BETTY   My kid.

HOLAHAN   The one you killed. Ah, yes, that Bert.

Music. A blonde appears out of the dark. She's very tough, very blowsy. A good sport. Her name is ROSALIE. *She wears a white spangly evening gown.*

ROSALIE   They're getting you for your lifestyle, kid. They can't stand it that you got the lifestyle of the future and they're stuck here in their little precincts.

BETTY   I'm being prosecuted for my lifestyle. You can't stand it that I got the lifestyle of the future and you're stuck here in your little precinct.

Rosalie embraces Betty and comforts her. Rosalie goes back into the dark.

HOLAHAN   Bert's body was found yesterday afternoon floating off an abandoned pier at the bottom of Charles Street in a particularly seedy part of Greenwich Village. The boy's head was found floating close by. No signs of sexual molestation. But the boy was not killed there. The murder took place someplace else. The body was taken and dumped off this abandoned pier notorious for sexual pickups between members shall we say of the same sex and for the exchange of narcotic goods exchanged between people so spaced out they don't know what sex they are. From the boy's school pass, we find where he lives on Christopher Street, a notorious street in the self-same Greenwich Village. We find evidence in the boy's apartment where he lives with his mother, we find evidences of blood in his own home. In the bathroom. The boy was murdered and decapitated in the bathroom of his own legal abode. The mother lived there with the boy. The mother is a hotsy-totsy we find out. The mother works in porno films.

BETTY Soft core.

HOLAHAN *Do Me Do Me Do Me Till It Falls Off* does not sound soft core to me. *Leather Sheets* does not sound soft core to me. Vaginal penetration recorded in medical detail by a sixteen-millimeter camera owned by Mafia people does not sound soft core to me.

BETTY That wasn't me in all of them. My sister worked in porno films. I was finishing up a contract she had made shortly before her death.

HOLAHAN And when you appear on *What's My Line*? How do you sign in, please?

BETTY I work in a travel agency.

HOLAHAN A fake travel agency.

Music. RAULITO, *a Cuban in a trench coat, appears out of the dark.*

RAULITO Honeymoon Holidays was not fake.

HOLAHAN Closed down for selling fraudulent trips—

RAULITO It don't harm nobody to start off a marriage with a good honeymoon.

Raulito goes back into the dark. Betty takes pills out of her pocket. Holahan knocks them out.

HOLAHAN No junkie shit here, baby.

BETTY They're Tums for my tummy, asshole. I don't want to throw up. If I do not throw up, it will somehow prove to me that I am not on your level, that I possess a strength, am the proud possessor of a dignity—

HOLAHAN   And yet Miss Dignity seems to appear in these loops. We raided Dirty Mort's on Forty-second Street. We ran the loops. I remembered your face from the loops when they brought you in. I had long said to myself what kind of person would allow another human being to urinate on her while a Mafia-run camera was whirring away. Little did I think, Miss Lifestyle of the Future, I would have the honor of having met you. As you see, I am a movie buff. Those films. These films. This doesn't look like anybody's sister to me. This looks coincidentally like you. Or maybe it's Gene Kelly in outtakes from *Singin' in the Rain*? What kind of human being allows herself to be treated in this way? I hate you, baby.

BETTY   No shit, Dick Tracy. I thought this was a love story.

HOLAHAN   When I was a kid my parents chained me to the piano so I'd play. I was a fat kid, too, so the chains had double purpose. The pressure of them would stop me eating and force me to play. I eat, baby. I eat the right amounts and I am thin and I play the piano very well. And I also know all about family hatred. I know that families are there to learn your deepest secrets and betray you with their intimacy. Your kid must've found out too much about you. Your kid, I'm beginning to see, cramped your style. Of course! Every kid thinks his mother is the Virgin Mary, for Christ's sake, and one day your kid sees the films you work in when you're not in the fake travel agency. I get it! And I find it a fantastic fact that a woman who gives head in twenty-five-cent loops should be in here for taking head. To get rid of the son's head that contained the eyes that saw her life.

BETTY   Are you nuts?

HOLAHAN   Because his eyes turned into these mason jars preserving the disgust at what you had become.

BETTY   I want out of here! (*She bangs on doors.*) That's not me in those films. That's my sister.

HOLAHAN   Oh sure. Your sister. Bring her in here. Testify for you.

BETTY   She's dead.

HOLAHAN   When?

BETTY   A year ago, last October.

Raulito appears.

RAULITO   Is that what happened to you?

Rosalie appears.

BETTY   She was walking on Hudson Street.

ROSALIE   I was just walking down on Hudson Street.

BETTY   A cyclist hit her.

HOLAHAN   And Raulito.

BETTY   He's dead.

Raulito and Rosalie happily go into the black, arm in arm.

HOLAHAN   You're a terrific dame to know. All the people connected to you via the avenue of blood die in one year. Maybe I'll go to Bangor, Maine, and dig your sister up.

BETTY   I'm really grateful to you.

HOLAHAN   The Grateful Dead. The noted rock group.

BETTY   I am alive, Detective. Because I am, I was going crazy from my son's death . . . When they came and told me the kid was dead, they could've fit me for a straitjacket at the same time they were fitting him for a shroud. You have actually taken my mind off it. My loathing for you replaces my grief. I mean, my fury is real. You're nuts.

HOLAHAN   Do you deny you made golden shower films where people urinated on you?

BETTY   That was my sister.

HOLAHAN   Oh, this is one of those movies where there's a good twin and an evil twin.

BETTY   You got movies on the brain. It must make life easy for you. You can just put anything you want into a movie and that explains everything.

HOLAHAN   I'm sorry, Betty. I look to the family. I go right to the scene of the crime between those shapely gams. The family, Betty.

BETTY   You're a class act, Detective. Detective Marvin Holahan. *Detective That's Entertainment Parts One and Two and Three and Four.* What are you? Some faggot out to get me because—

HOLAHAN   I know everything about you.

BETTY   You don't know nothing about me except that I posed for some sleazy pictures and who cares. But I know about you. They chained you to a piano so you wouldn't eat and you would play. And you do both and you're a good boy. A lot of things have happened to me, but nobody ever chained me to a piano and you know what? I didn't throw up. I can look you right in the eye. I didn't throw up. I won.

The interrogation room goes dark. Lights come up on Rosalie. A piano swings into view. Rosalie sings to us in the audience. She's really good-natured, has a sweil voice, moves like a stripper.

ROSALIE   Hey Stay A While
In the crook of my arms
All you got to do is
Look in my arms
And you'll see Home Sweet Home
I'll invest in a doormat
Hey Home Sweet Home
We'll test the mattress
Our arms are sinuous
All performances are continuous
Hey Stay A While
Feel the smile in my arms
And the smile's in my arms
All for you
Sit back / Relax
Cool brow / Tension slacks
Hey Stay A While
My arms are filled with
What the whole world lacks
Hey Stay A While

Being dead is not the worst thing in the world. Is there life after death? I dare ask the question: Is there life before death? The good thing about being dead is at least you know where you stand. You have one piece of information in life and you think life means this. Then you get a new piece of info and everything you knew means something else. The scary thing about death is how comfortable it is. Finally giving in to the drowning. Life was always wriggling out of my hands like a fish you thought you had all hooked and ready to pop in the pan. Was there ever a day I didn't at one point say, "Hey, when will life end?" Flashback! A new scene starring the boy who would soon be murdered.

BERT, *a fourteen-year-old kid, swaggers on, wearing earphones. He dances to silent music. He wears about a dozen wristwatches.*

ROSALIE This scene you are about to see contains information completely unknown to the boy's mother, my sister. Information unknown to Captain Marvin Holahan of the Sixth Precinct Homicide. Those two people in the course of their lives never learned the information you are about to receive right now. This scene takes place in the Parthenon. Not the one in Greece that's the cradle of all civilization. Hell, baby, I'm talking the Parthenon Luncheonette on West Eleventh Street and Bleecker in Greenwich Village. This scene takes place four weeks before this boy, my nephew, will be murdered.

A booth and table and chairs come in. Bert sits in the booth, his arm around one of the girls. Another boy, DONNY, has his sleeves rolled up and is wearing a lot of wristwatches. The girls lean forward. The kids are roughly thirteen, fourteen.

BERT It's so easy.

DONNY Easy he says.

BERT You stand on Christopher Street.

DONNY I got to wait in the tub.

BERT Pretty soon the guy stops.

DONNY The tub gets cold. You got a cold ass waiting in the tub.

BERT You noticed him 'cause he's walked back and forth a few times looking at you.

DONNY All the things a tub can be. A coffin. I pretend I'm in a coffin.

JOANNE Does he look at you like you're a girl?

DONNY I pretend I'm in a boat.

JOANNE Do they really look fruity?

DONNY Sometimes they're in cars. Not fruity cars, but Pontiacs. Oldsmobiles.

JOANNE Fruits driving Pontiacs?

DONNY I pretend I'm in a car.

MARGIE I could see a Chevrolet. Chevrolets are fruity.

BERT Not the Sixty-five Chevy, Joanne. Holy shit, Joanne, I look at you sometimes and I say—

JOANNE It was Margie who said it.

BERT You were looking at her, agreeing with her.

JOANNE Don't get mad at me. I'm sorry, Bert?

BERT I don't like the two of you hanging around together. She's dragging you down. We all got to protect each other. Make each other better. Margie's dragging you down.

JOANNE She's not cheap.

MARGIE I only felt cheap once in my life. Charlie Ebbermann said he'd give me ten cents to let him touch me in the cloakroom. This is the fifth grade. The sixth grade. So I do. Big deal. Then I hear later, Charlie Ebbermann is paying a girl from the public school a quarter to take out

16

her glass eye and let him look in. I saw him and I said, Look, Ebbermann, you can take your dime back and I threw it at him.

BERT (*Calls*)   Hey, could we get a Coke or something? A toasted bran?

DONNY   Bert brings the fruit upstairs. His mother's away. He leads them into the bathroom. I'm happy 'cause I can finally get out of the fucking tub. I hear the voices behind the shower curtain. I make sure the shower curtain's shut. I see the fruit's shadow on the shower curtain. (*Takes a monkey wrench out of his jacket*) I leap out of the tub and bang the guy on the head with the monkey wrench. He don't know what hit him.

BERT   I pull the watch off. Take the wallet. We roll 'im to the door. Push 'im out in the hall. We piss in the corner.

DONNY   Piss on the guy.

BERT   Then I knock on the door next door. Mrs. Pantoni, I tell her, there's another drunk broke in. He peed on the floor. I spill some wine on him. She calls the cops. The cops come and clear the guy out.

MARGIE   They don't ever report you?

BERT   You don't have big ears, but you're a real dumbo, Margie. I don't want you hanging around with her, Joanne.

JOANNE   I got to have some friends, Bert.

BERT   You got me.

JOANNE   You swear?

BERT (*With his arm around Joanne*)   Who they gonna report? Some fairy tries to pick up a fourteen-year-old?

17

JOANNE   All that ticking. Your arm is so noisy.

DONNY   You have all the fun. I got to stick in the tub. You wait in the tub for a while. You see how much fun it is in a fucking tub.

BERT   Some fairy in a Chevrolet with Jersey plates is gonna pick you up? I want to make some money, not scare 'em away.

DONNY   That's right. I'd scare 'em away. (*He makes a monster face and waves his wrench.*)

JOANNE   Let me wind your watches? You read in the papers today about the lady in Forest Hills who died and they couldn't figure out how she died? She was healthy. Well, you know how she died?

BERT   Donny hit her over the head with his monkey.

DONNY   That's right. I hit her over the head with my monkey.

MARGIE   Would you let her tell her story?

BERT   (*Calls*)   You burning that bran muffin?

JOANNE   She had this beautiful beehive hairdo that she wore. Really intricate. Curls. Upswept. Spit curls. And she didn't want to damage it because her hairdo was really a work of art. *Hairdo* magazine was considering her for a feature. And she kept spraying her hairdo with hair spray so her hairdo wouldn't get hurt when she went to sleep at night and you know what happened? In Forest Hills, Queens, they traced black widow spiders escaped and hid in her hair. Somehow they ended up in her hair because they like dark places and the hair spray made this shield like Gardol on the toothpaste commercial where the decay can't get through the toothpaste. And the black widow spiders got trapped within her hairdo in this wall of hair spray and got panicked and couldn't get out and ate their way through her skull. Bit her in the skull to get out and that's how she died.

Bert and Joanne neck.

DONNY Bert?

MARGIE Can I have a bite of that bran muffin?

DONNY Bert? Is your mother at work?

JOANNE Bran is supposed to be the secret of life.

BERT You feel like getting another wristwatch?

MARGIE How'd that woman do her hair?

Bert and Donny go. Joanne begins demonstrating. The lights come down on the luncheonette and up on Rosalie, by her piano. She prepares herself for the next scene, putting on a brief kimono.

ROSALIE Flashback. Eighteen months ago. I was still among the living. How my sister and nephew came to New York in the first place.

Rosalie's apartment. A sink, a table, a chair, a daybed strewn with clothes, a vanity. Rosalie's putting on makeup and drinking coffee and snorting a few hits of cocaine to get her day started. Betty and Bert appear. Betty looks different from what we have seen before. Eighteen months ago she was very plain. Very nervous.

BETTY Rosalie, you got to come home. You're growing up not knowing your family. Your nephew. Our mother.

Bert shyly looks out from behind his mother.

ROSALIE Hiya, kid. Want a snort?

19

BETTY   Tell her, Bert.

Bert steps forward, all rehearsed.

BERT   Bangor, Maine, is about the greatest place I know. It's not like the old days when nothing was there. Bangor, Maine, is the home of one of the world's busiest airports.

He holds out a pennant marked BANGOR.

ROSALIE   He's great.

BERT   Bangor, Maine, is the center of the chartered jet service that takes Americans to all parts of the globe on budget flights.

ROSALIE   You done good, Betty.

BETTY   Rosalie, Bangor is so interesting. You meet people from all over the world who are laying over. Lots of times they're fogged in and you get to hear about their travels and I sell souvenirs and there's an opening in the cocktail lounge. You could sing. You'd meet such interesting people. I pray for snow. I pray for fog. All the things that used to make life so dismal in Bangor are now the exact things that make it so interesting.

ROSALIE   Honeybunch, you're hearing about the world. But hearing about it don't put no notches on anyone's pistol. I'm doing. Bert, would you go out onto Christopher Street to the Li-Lac-Chocolate store and request about a pound of kisses?

She gives Bert money. Bert goes.

BETTY   Bert, you be careful. Is it safe out there?

ROSALIE   Honeybunch, I get this call last week, would I be interested appearing in a film. Sure, why not.

20

BETTY   He's never been to a city before.

ROSALIE   I report to a motel on Forty-second Street and
Eleventh Avenue. Way west. Take elevator to the sixth
floor. Knock. Go in. Floodlights. A camera. Workmen
setting up. The real thing! A man said, "You the girl? Get
your duds off. Sink into the feathers and go to it." Holy
shit, they're loading the cameras and I'm naked and
nobody's really paying attention. They say, "You all set?"
Sure, why not. Lights. Camera. Action. And a door I
thought was a closet opens up and it's from another room
and a gorilla leaps out with a slit in his suit and this
enormous erection and the gorilla jumps on me.
Honeybunch, there's no surprises like that in Maine. And
we're going at it and I can't believe it and after about five
minooties, the director yells "Cut!" and the gorilla rolls off
me, takes off his gorilla head, and it's Harry Reems from
Deep Throat and *The Devil in Miss Jones*. What an honor to
meet you, sir, I said. Christ! Go back to Bangor, Maine!
Honey, you should move in with me. Get yourself
unsaddled from Momma and that house and airports.

BETTY   It's our family.

Rosalie dresses for work and takes a few snorts.

ROSALIE   Honeybaby, start your own family. I started my
own family. I've got a family motto. "She Travels Fastest
Who Travels Alone." I live here on Christopher Street. A
lovely building. Lovely neighbors. Leave you alone.
Nobody knows me. I don't know anybody. I'm flying high.
I'm working for a travel agency. Dawn's Promising Star
Travel Agency. Founder and sponsor of Honeymoon
Holidays. No charter jets for me. When I travel, which shall
be soon, I'll be traveling first class not out of Bangor but

right out of old JFK. Wait till you meet my boss, Raulito. Take it back. Erase those tapes. You'll never meet him. I'd show you my life, you'd get so jealous, you'd want to move right in and take me over. You can't have me. You can have yourself but you can't have me. Ditch the kid. He comes from a whole other rotten period of your life. Erase those tapes. Get rid of him. I got a pull-out sofa. Move in. We can have some laughs.

BETTY I've got lots of laughs in Bangor. When it isn't raining, it's snowing. I meet boys at the airport, but they end up taking planes. Momma sits by the TV singing "Rosalie, My Darling" over and over and over. Aside from that, everything is okay.

ROSALIE Listen, send the kid back. There's an extra key.

BETTY Momma sent me down here to bring you back.

ROSALIE You just wire a little wire to Momma. Hey, Momma, send me a change-of-address card. I get lonely, Honeybunch. We could have some laughs. I'm proud of my life and I'd like to show it off to you. We're young.

Bert enters with a bag of chocolates.

ROSALIE Hiya, kid. We were just talking about you.

BERT Kisses!

The lights go out on Bert and Betty in Rosalie's apartment. Rosalie steps in time to the very jazzy piano music.

ROSALIE So I walk out on Christopher, cut down on Bleecker to walk to work, and I'm just jazzing along Hudson Street, and you know where that Ristorante Rigoletto is that the papers gave eighteen tureens to and they got limousines parked out front and I happen to know the chef sprays fresh herbs on the canned Boyardee, but what the hell, it's overpriced, out of the way, they treat you like shit, and Uptown loves it.

A cyclist appears behind her wearing a mask, goggles, helmet, and spandex, holding a bicycle with a broken chain over his head. He advances slowly, threateningly, toward her.

ROSALIE   Well, I'm being so specific because it's just at that very location that a ten-speed yellow Raleigh bike bears down on me. I apparently splattered up against the window of the Ristorante Rigoletto like a pizza that suddenly appeared on the menu. My last thoughts were of Betty moving down to New York. I won her. Revenge on our Momma. I was feeling very happy.

The sound of a crash. Rosalie sinks to the ground, slowly caressing the MASKED MAN's *body as she falls. The Masked Man glares at us, never lowering his bicycle.*

MASKED MAN   I don't give a shit if she's dead. Who's gonna fix my bike? The chain is off my bike! Who's gonna pay for that? Give me her bag. She owes me money. Life belongs to the living. I don't give a shit if she just died. She should've looked. I am traveling. I am moving. Who's gonna pay for my bike? Chocolate? That's all she's got in the fucking bag? Chocolate kisses? How am I supposed to fix my bike with chocolate kisses? She deserves to die.

He stomps her bag of kisses, walks off into the black. Rosalie sits up and sings.

ROSALIE   Was that Mister Right?
If it was, I'll let it pass.
The right Mister Right

That funky-looking skunk
Put me kerplunk on my ass

I thought Mister Right
Would have a little more couth.
He'd come on a white charger
Say hi-de-hi to my charm
And vo-de-oh to my youth

The bright music continues under:

ROSALIE So Betty Yearn, newly arrived from Bangor,
Maine, stays in New York to settle my estate along with my
hash. She moves into my apartment, she takes over my job.
I'm not even cool in the grave yet, and she's got my job.
She moves into my life. Betty Yearn's first day eighteen
months ago in the Dawn's Promising Star Travel Agency. A
division of Honeymoon Holidays.

*The music turns Latin. A travel agency appears: a desk, a telephone,
piles of newspapers, lots of telephone books, a cassette recorder that
contains tapes of cheering and applause. Betty is dressed in a bland
outfit for her first day at work. Raulito wears what happens to be a
gold lamé evening gown over his business suit and still looks mucho
macho. Raulito is knockout handsome, like a 1940s leading man with
a pompadour and diamond rings. He carries an armful of Sunday's
papers.*

RAULITO You take the *Daily News*. You take the Sunday
Times. Not the financial section. Not the sports section.

BETTY There's so many sections.

RAULITO The engagement section.

BETTY The society page.

RAULITO You look up the name of the father, the man who
is paying for the wedding.

BETTY   Mr. and Mrs. Bernard Culkin of Corona and Point Lookout announce the engagement of their daughter, Lillibet—

RAULITO   Stop right there. You look in the phone book. Not the Manhattan phone book.

BETTY   So I look up Corona in . . . there are so many phone books. I've only been here a few days.

RAULITO   Corona is in Queens.

BETTY   Culkin. B-B-B-B-B-B . . . Bernard.

RAULITO   Don't *show* it to me. Copy the phone number down on the pad.

BETTY   I swear to you, I'm generally very good at writing numbers.

RAULITO   Check the bride-to-be's name.

BETTY   Lillibet.

RAULITO   See what Lillibet does. Where Lillibet is employed.

BETTY   "Educated at St. John's University."

RAULITO   Your sister was like streaks of lightning here.

BETTY   "Is employed as a researcher at Mutual Life."

RAULITO   So she should be home at five-thirty. Mark down to call her at?

BETTY   Five-forty-five?

RAULITO   Five-thirty-one!

BETTY   Nice to have a few minutes to get your coat off.

RAULITO   Your late and more and more lamented sister would have that phone ringing off the hook the instant Lillibet Culkin Corona Queens stuck her key in the door.

BETTY   Fine.

RAULITO   If I may be so bold, petals on a pool drifting, you want a travel brochure back to Bangor?

BETTY   No! I feel my sister wanted me to have this job.

RAULITO   No hard feelings. We can be friends. If I'm ever in Bangor, God forbid, I'll look you up. Is the job too hard for you?

BETTY   I can do it.

RAULITO   Then honey through the comb sifting, you must be prepared to play Follow the Leader. Miss Lisa Staminelli to wed law student. Bayside, Queens. Father Frank Staminelli. Presented to society the Gotham Ball. You have the Queens phone book. Zut zut zut zut *zut* you have the number. You dial it. (*He accomplishes this task in a dazzlingly quick stroke.*) This is where my Rosalie was brilliant. (*He talks into the phone.*) Miss Lisa Staminelli. Is she there? Is this she? This is she? The noted debutante? I am talking to her. Ohhhhh, Miss Staminelli, this is *Bride's Magazine* calling. Of course I'm breathless. Are you sitting down? Miss Staminelli, you've won our lottery. An all-expense-paid honeymoon for two to Paradise Cove. Two weeks! (*He clicks on the cassette—cheers and applause—then turns it off.*)

BETTY   Two weeks?

RAULITO   Yes! For you and Mr. Right— (*He checks the paper.*) Bruce Mandrake. How did I know? Darling, we here at

Bride's Magazine know *tout*! If we didn't know who was getting married, we wouldn't know if the world would keep spinning. We need families and families are love and love pulled your number out of the lottery. Fate wanted you and your new husband, Mr. Mandrake—is he the magician?—to have this honeymoon. Do you think it's possible, God, we know you're so busy, would it be possible for you and Señor Right to stop down to our office and pick up your honeymoon? Fourteenth Street. 618 West. Ninth floor. The Honeymoon Holidays Building. Could you and Bruce toddle on down here any night after work, say seven? We could finalize arrangements for the honeymoon? Some forms to sign.

The piano plays a tango.

RAULITO   Then you could have a lovely evening in the Village. Greenwich Village. Chianti. Pasta. Discuss your future. Discuss your honeymoon. It's all luck and love is luck and you're the luckiest girl in the world, Lisa. The past shows us the mistakes we made. The future's the place where we won't make them again. Dreams are the fuel for reality. A new family is coming into the world! Oh God! Grab the Now! The Now is all quicksilver and mercury. The Now is diamonds. Can I make an appointment for you? Lucky you! I could squeeze you in tomorrow at seven-ten. Oh, Lisa, you've made all of us so happy at *Bride's Magazine*. (*He clicks on the cassette of cheering.*) See you tomorrow. (*He hangs up and clicks off the cassette.*) You're the bait, baby. You lure them in here. You decorate the hook. *I* make the sale.

BETTY   Everybody falls for it?

RAULITO Sometimes a black eye. Every now and then a death threat. But, Sweetness and Light, if I can make one sale a week, that is two trips to the Caribbean, I can make out all right. Besides what is living without a little danger?

BETTY Do they ever call *Bride's Magazine*?

RAULITO Only the smart ones and they're not exactly our clientele.

BETTY Could we be sued?

RAULITO By who?

BETTY *Bride's Magazine.*

RAULITO For what?

BETTY I don't want to go to jail. My life is beginning. I don't want to be arrested.

RAULITO Hey, hey, hey. Evidence obtained by wiretap is illegal. Can't be introduced into court. What planet are you from anyway, baby?

BETTY What borough is the moon in?

RAULITO The moon is the fifty-first state. Hawaii. Alaska. The moon. Did you see the moon last night? Like a little Turkish flag waving in the sky? I saluted.

BETTY Why do you dress that way?

RAULITO That is exactly what your sister Rosalie said to me the first time we met. We would curl up on her pull-out sleep sofa, now *your* pull-out sleep sofa, and I would tell her my dream to one night turn on the TV and hear the late show say, "And tonight our guest is *me!*"

Bright show-biz music. He clicks on the cassette of people cheering.

RAULITO Thank you, Johnny. I'm from Cuba. We lived on
the other side of the island. From Havana.

*Then the music turns latin. Raulito sits beside the desk as if he were
the guest on the* Tonight Show *and Betty the host.*

RAULITO Poor. You never saw such poor. We were so poor
that. You know those jokes? He was so fat *that.* She was so
dumb *that.* Well, we were so *poor* that. When I was wearing
rags, I was running around naked! This part of Cuba that
we called the country, I think any normal-thinking person
would call it the jungle! Occasionally, a magazine would
appear in our village and I'd see the pictures of evening
gowns and spangles and barrettes in the hair and these high
heels. I didn't know till later that was what women wore. I
thought that was rich people. I thought if you were rich and
lived in the city or lived in America that was what the
average American family hung around in. The revolution
came. I saw Che Guevara this close. We left Cuba. We got
to Florida. Where I found out that those uniforms with
diamonds and lace did not belong to the typical American
man. But a few years ago, I was shopping in the Salvation
Army for a winter coat and I came upon this real Rita
Hayworth special. A beautiful 1940s evening gown for
twenty-five cents. I bought it. Why not? The dreams we
have as kids, they're the dreams we never get over. I put it
on over my suit. I feel rich. I feel successful.

*Raulito begins to spin. The gold dress flares out. He advances on
Betty, now waving his dress like Dracula's cape, then like a matador's
cape in front of her. Betty is terrified.*

RAULITO I feel I can get out of the jungle and get to
America and twirl and twirl. Feeling good outside I start to
feel good inside. I start Honeymoon Holidays. I want to
start a family. I want to start a life. Betty, your sister went

29

with me. Your sister would let me dance with her first. Then she would let me sleep with her after and dreams would come out of our heads like little Turkish moons. We would salute. Betty?

BETTY (*Getting back to work*)   It's about five-thirty. I'd better call Lillibet.

RAULITO   You like the name Lillibet?

BETTY   It's a name. People have names. I take the Queens phone book.

RAULITO   Do you know what Queen Elizabeth's secret name is? If you were in her royal family, what you would call her?

BETTY   Elizabeth. They'd call her Elizabeth. They'd call her Queen Elizabeth. Elizabeth is short for Queen Elizabeth.

RAULITO   They'd call her Lillibet.

BETTY   I thought I was safe when I came in here, when I met you at my sister's funeral I thought, This guy's a weirdo but I'll be safe.

RAULITO   Lillibet is the queen's secret name. What Prince Philip calls her when they're alone. I read that in *People* magazine. *Alone* must mean also in the royal bed. Prince Philip calls over to her: Lillibet? He turns on the royal radio station. A little English Latin music comes on the royal radio.

Music: mambo.

RAULITO   I should call you Lillibet. Tell me your story? Unfold yourself to me?

BETTY   I'm Betty. Betty's short for Elizabeth. I'm a Betty. That's all I am. I have no story. I'm no guest on any talk show. No story. I am a middle-aged woman. I'm a young

30

girl. I'm regular. Quiet. Normal. Human person. (*She is shaking violently. She plays the cheering on the cassette and dials the telephone.*) Is Miss Lillibet Culkin there? Hi! This is *Bride's Magazine* calling. The lottery of love twirled and stopped at . . . Oh? The wedding is off? The groom is dead? Head injuries? Attacked by a monkey wrench? Greenwich Village? Beaten brutally? Watch stolen? I don't care. Don't tell me your troubles. You won a honeymoon. That's all I want to tell you. That's all. (*She clicks off the cassette and hangs up.*) Lillibet Culkin. Corona, Queens. I don't want the job. I can't handle the job. I'm not my sister. I am not Rosalie. I can't do her job. I'm not Lillibet. I'm not Queen Elizabeth. I'm nobody. I'm me. I can't do the job. I don't want the job.

Raulito has picked her up. He tangos her away into the dark. Rosalie appears.

ROSALIE   Frightened of you
    All of these years
    Never secure
    In your embrace
    Sleep through the night
    Dream that I'm dead
    Feeling your weight
    There in the bed

    One little bag
    Never unpacked
    Hidden away
    In case
    I get the nerve
    One day to leave
    Finally that fact
    To face

31

What's getting me through my life?
What's my excuse inside?
What's keeping me in my life?
The molehill of lust or the mountain of pride?

Forgive me, my dear
A slip of the tongue
Forget what I said
Erase
I meant to say
My life is brightened by you
The darkness whitened by you
Each moment heightened by you
My life enlightened by you
But not I'm frightened of you
Forgive me
I'm sorry
Don't hit me
I love you

A year and a half later. Eighteen count 'em eighteen
months. My sister has moved into my life. It's like two days
before the boy's murder.

*The lights reveal Betty and Raulito necking, passionately. He has
gathered his evening gown up under his trench coat. Betty is a lot more
sure of herself in the last months since we've seen her, and a lot sexier.*

Rosalie observes the scene.

*Rosalie's apartment. Bert sits on a red beanbag, winding watches.
Betty comes in the room. She takes off her dress. She stands in a slip.*

BETTY   I bought this new dress today. You like it? (*She takes
another dress out of a shopping bag.*) Or do you like this one?
(*She puts on Rosalie's robe.*) What do you think moving

32

maybe to Miami? I got a chance finally after eighteen months at Raulito's. A free trip for two. National Airlines. There's a lot of cities we could fly to. LA. Round-trip ticket but we could just stay. Stop winding all those watches. I never saw anyone for finding so many watches. Find 'em and wind 'em. That's your name. The watch monster. That's what I gave birth to. Can't you say anything? Jesus. Who'd've thought you'd grow up to be your father. To have to live through all that again. Can't you say anything?

BERT How's Honeymoon Holidays?

BETTY Raulito called me a professional today. He gave me a gold star. (*She picks up the phone.*) Miss Mary Louise Nicholson? The lottery of love twirled and twirled and stopped at your number. It don't hurt to start a marriage with a good honeymoon. (*She slams the phone down.*)

BERT Did you and Daddy have a good honeymoon?

BETTY If I had a good honeymoon, you think I'd be working at Honeymoon Holidays?

BERT You going to marry Raulito?

BETTY Raulito already has a wife and about nineteen children. He gave me this butterfly pin. It was his grandmother's. (*She bends it.*) Now you bend it. I don't want anybody doing nice for me.

Bert bends the pin. Betty throws the pin away.

BETTY I don't want anybody giving me presents. I don't want to be reminded what I missed out on. We should've had a family. We could've had a family. A regular dynasty. I had a family. I should've passed one on to you. If we'd had a

33

family, we'd go to the movies and eat at McDonald's and take summer trips to Maine to see your grandmother and see free Shakespeare in the park and take long rides on the subway to the Bronx Zoo and the Brooklyn Botanicals. If we had a family, things'd be a lot different around here.

BERT   Why can't we go do all those things now? They're all free.

BETTY   Because they're things families do together. Because they remind me how I screwed up my life. If we don't do nothing, I don't get reminded. But I don't want to turn you against your father. I want you to love your father. Your father was a god. Your father was the handsomest man I ever saw. Your father had a body you could see through his clothes. Your father had shoulders out to here and a waist you could clasp your thumb and index finger around. A brain of a fucking wizard. He could remember telephone numbers. Addresses. He could remember lottery numbers and the social security numbers of people he met a hundred years ago. Serial numbers of guys he was in the army with. He was kind of creepy when you come to think of it.

BERT   He sounds great.

BETTY   We bumped into an old army buddy and your father said, "I remember you. 19769982." The guy says, "Hey, why'd you remember my serial number?" Your father says, "Hold on. I haven't been thinking about you all these years. I just happen to have that kind of memory."

BERT   So why's he forgot where we live?

BETTY   A blind spot. He forgot you. He forgot me. For a guy with a memory. What I think is us living on Christopher Street. Ever since the Catholic Church said St. Christopher

34

doesn't exist, maybe he thinks Christopher Street doesn't exist either.

BERT But you left him.

BETTY I didn't mind him, well, I did, him putting my head down the toilet and flushing it. But you. When he put your head down the toilet and flushed it, I said that's it. And I told him to leave.

BERT I have dreams sometimes of water rushing by me.

BETTY That comes from your father putting your head down the toilet.

BERT I think I'll join the navy when I can. The submarine service.

BETTY You been seeing too many Walt Disney movies.

JOANNE (*Runs in, breathless*) You know what my mother told me today? A lady in her office knew a lady who died and they couldn't find a reason why she died. She was healthy.

BETTY I don't want to hear any more black widow spiders. You get me?

JOANNE This isn't black widow spiders. This is the truth. This lady died and they traced all her steps and they found she had gone to Korvette's department store and on her dead body they found her wearing a beautiful Indian blouse with pieces of mirror sewn in it.

BETTY Sounds pretty. Korvette's?

JOANNE And they traced all her steps and went to Korvette's and opened the drawer where the Indian blouses came from and they reached in and the detective pulled back his hand because it almost got bit by a cobra. Which is what happened to the lady. These blouses had come in from India. And cobra eggs had got woven in beneath the mirrors while the blouses were being made and the cobra eggs hatched from the heat of being mailed over here and the lady reached her hand in the drawer and got bitten and died.

BETTY   Where is this woman? How come you always have these friends who are getting bit by black widow spiders? Bit by cobras.

BERT   It was her mother's friend.

BETTY   I don't believe her mother.

Bert puts his arms around Joanne.

BERT   Then you don't believe me. Are you calling me a liar?

BETTY   I don't want you hanging around together. I don't want any more stories about black widow spiders and black widow cobras. I'm up to here with it.

Joanne runs out.

BETTY   And you be careful with her. I don't want any fourteen-year-old fathers living in my house. I'm not ready to be a grandmother yet.

BERT   You old hag. You old crone. I know how old you are. You're thirty-six and you're gonna die soon and I'm fourteen and I'm going to live forever. I hate you. You're going to die. You know what I want for Christmas? You in a coffin under a Christmas tree. Why did Aunt Rosalie have to die? Why couldn't you be the one that bicycle hit. Maybe that guy is around right now speeding down streets looking for you.

BETTY   You know why you can't hurt me? 'Cause I have X-ray eyes and I can see right into your heart.

BERT Bullshit.

BETTY Remember that old man with the pushcart in Bangor who called out "Old clothes"? You used to follow him for hours. What did you do with that filthy old man? Old clothes. I place my X-ray eyes over you and I see deep in you. Old Clothes. Old Clothes. Old Clothes.

BERT Don't say that.

BETTY Old clothes. Old rags. Old rats. X–ray eyes.

BERT Don't say that! Don't say that!

BETTY Don't have to say it. I feel it. I'm being very quiet and saying it to myself over and over. (*Wordless: Old Clothes.*)

Bert hits her. She hits him back.

BERT Shut up! Shut up!

BETTY I'm not saying anything. (*Wordless: Old Clothes.*)

BERT It's what you're thinking. Can't think that. Stop! Stop!

BETTY I love thinking. I can think anything I want.

BERT I've killed people.

BETTY Don't make me laugh.

BERT I haven't killed them. Donny's killed them.

BETTY There you are. You couldn't hurt a fly. I don't mean that as a compliment. I mean that as a truth. You could not wound a mosquito. If David and Goliath had a fight, Goliath would reach down and squeeze your head like a seedless grape.

BERT   I lure them up here while you're away and Donny and I kill them. Hit them on the head with the monkey. Take their watches. Roll them out in the hall. They don't dare call the cops on us. I can so hurt a fly.

BETTY   (*Slaps him*)   Lure? Where'd you learn a word like *lure*?

BERT   I know a lot of words.

BETTY   There's a whole series of murders going around.

BERT   Maybe that's me.

BETTY   Decapitations.

BERT   What's that?

BETTY   Down at all these rough bars down by the river. Raulito told me at work they find people with heads chopped off. The police don't bother to check them out. It's not worth the trouble. You're not part of those murders, are you? I told you to stay away from those docks, you little faggot.

BERT   What's decap— decap—

BETTY   Chop their heads off!

BERT   I didn't do that! I swear! I'm just into watches. Money. The monkey wrench. I don't think any of them ever died. I swear.

A man appears at the door—a large man, carefully dressed in a wrinkled white linen suit, Panama hat. He carries flowers.

BETTY   (*Terrified*)   Is this one of them?

MAN   Betty? Betty Mandible?

BETTY   (*A pause*)   I was.

38

BERT Are you the police?

MAN You got married.

BETTY Oh yes. My husband here and I are very happy. Some people say he's too young. I say why not?

MAN Hello, Betty.

BERT My mother says go away. She doesn't know you. Ma? Is this guy bothering you?

BETTY I know who you are.

MAN I was hoping you would.

BETTY In Bangor. Summer of—

MAN Nineteen years ago. I'm Durwood Peach.

BETTY Durwood Peach. The Good Humor Man. Pushing that white ice-cream truck.

DURWOOD Name like a flavor of ice cream. The special may be blueberry ripple but I'm pushing the peach.

BETTY You were from North—

DURWOOD South.

BETTY Carolina. You came up to Bangor, to visit your aunt.

DURWOOD Can I sit down for a minute? Excuse me for not being on my toes more. Oh, I have been driving. I drove from South Carolina straight up to Bangor, Maine, and looked up your name in the phone book. Your mother answered. She told me your swell sister had passed on. She told me you were here. You were the one I wanted. I got back in my car and drove from Maine nonstop here to Christopher Street. So this is Greenwich Village. Sure is lively. Mexican restaurant and a Chinese restaurant and an Indian restaurant all on one block. A lot of variety. Your mother didn't mention you had a little boy. Is he yours?

BERT I'm hers.

BETTY Why are you here?

DURWOOD See. Now I should have said that soon as I arrived. I never forgot you nineteen years ago and even though we never talked much and you had other boyfriends and you and me never went out, I have recently realized you are the only girl I ever loved, ever will love. My doctor gave me a note saying all this was true.

BETTY Doctor?

DURWOOD I been in a hospital and I got out and I been going to a doctor and you appeared to me like a holy movie when the Blessed Virgin appears and tells the holy children what to do. You appeared in my analysis. Here's the note.

BETTY Thank you. (*She takes the note.*)

DURWOOD Now my knees are shaking. I'm gonna faint.

BERT Should I call the police?

DURWOOD No! I'm all right. It's all the driving from South Carolina to Bangor, Maine, back to New York. Betty, I love you. I'll always love you. I've never loved anyone else. I've told my wife. She understands. She's written a note to you giving me up to you.

BETTY (*Reads*) "Dear Betty. I surrender all rights to Durwood heartbroken and bereft as that leaves me."

DURWOOD My grandfather, the only surviving member of my natural family, the head of the clan, welcomes you into

40

the family. I'm rich, Betty. I've got a farm and I lease it out to a racetrack and I make lots of money. Here's a thousand dollars in newly minted ten-dollar bills as a sign of faith. You remember me. I didn't have to introduce myself. I thought I'd have to introduce myself. That's a good sign. You remember me.

BERT   You want me to get my monkey? Bang him down on his head? I can get Donny down here.

BETTY   I never even kissed you.

DURWOOD   To pursue the unattainable. My doctor says that's my problem.

BETTY   The unattainable I'm afraid I must remain.

DURWOOD   No, you won't. I won't lie to you. I have been sick. And to be cured, I must once in my life obtain the unobtainable or I will die. I'm staying at the Dixie Hotel on West Forty-second Street. (*He takes a stack of bills from his jacket and places it on the table*.) I'll return there now and leave this one thousand dollars to show my good faith. I'll leave these photos of my farm and all that you'll be mistress of. A mountain. A river. Caves that are closed to the public. I'll give you time to peruse my offer and would like to ask your permission to call tomorrow night after which time perhaps we could leave immediately. You cannot escape from me or the power of my mind. We will begin a family. I'll be cured. We'll be happy. All these years. I'll be back tomorrow evening at six p.m. with my bags packed. I'll make a reservation at the Mexican restaurant for two.

BERT   For three.

DURWOOD   For two, Betty. You and me.

BETTY   I don't think you need reservations at Taco Trolley.

DURWOOD   Until tomorrow, Betty. Your mother's angry at you. She said she sent you down here to bring your sister back and you never returned. She said she had messages for you. She said get in touch. If I can bring you together, you and your mother, that'll be doing good. My doctor will be so happy. He said if you really want her, you'll find her. I didn't have to call. You were home. One of the largest cities in the world. You were here. Now I'm here. I'll be back tomorrow. The special is blueberry. But I'm pushing the peach.

Durwood goes. Bert has been counting the money Durwood left behind.

BETTY   I got to sit down.

BERT   You think it's counterfeit? You bend the face in half on two bills and if they fit together, the two faces into one face, that proves it's not counterfeit.

BETTY   I remember him.

BERT   You must have been the prettiest girl around that summer.

BETTY   I was pretty. But not this pretty. Do you think maybe he's telling the truth? South Carolina? Should I go? Maybe he does have money. Get us out of here. Who cares if he's a nut. It's amazing how a little tomorrow can make up for a whole lot of yesterday. It sounds like one of those uplift songs in a musical comedy. (*She sings.*) "It's amazing how a little tomorrow . . ."

BERT (*Sings*)   "Makes up for a whole lot of yesterday."

BETTY "It's amazing how a little tomorrow." Do you have a joint? A jay? Don't do lies to me. I found them in the Saltine box the last time.

BERT This time I hid the dope in the one place you'd never look.

BETTY Stop making with the funnies . . . I want to keep this moment. I feel it going away already and I'm hanging on to it. Don't go away, magic moment. I'll be right there.

BERT The one place you'd never look.

BETTY I give up.

BERT The broom closet.

BETTY You're right. The one place I'd never look. I like giant dustballs. It gives me a flavor of the Old West.

They sit on the daybed and light up. Rosalie appears and sings one of those rousing uplifting songs of a musical comedy.

ROSALIE It's amazing how a little tomorrow
Can make up for a whole lot of yesterday
It's amazing how a little tomorrow
Can make up for a whole lot of yesterday

Yesterday was dreary
Clocks kept on crawling
Now the future's cheery
How thrilling, how enthralling

It's amazing how a little tomorrow
Can recompense an awful lot of sorrow
So get yourself a little tomorrow
And wake up from those awful yesterdays.
It's amazing how a little tomorrow

Can recompense an awful lot of sorrow
So get yourself a little tomorrow
And wake up from those awful yesterdays.
Shake up all those bore-filled yester-
Make up those unlawful yesterdays.

*She inhales the smoke from the joint, bows, and goes into the
darkness. Bert and Betty sit on the daybed.*

BETTY   The first time I ever smoked pot, I was in a bar in
Rhode Island with my girlfriend.

BERT (*Bombed by the joint*)   The summer you met Durwood?

BETTY   No, after. This guy asked us if we wanted to smoke
reefers and my girlfriend said, "Only if you promise we'll
turn into sex-crazed nymphomaniacs who won't be held
responsible for any of their activities."

A man appears upstage, dressed like a beatnik.

BETTY   And the man said . . .

DOPE KING (*Striking a match*)   Results guaranteed.

BETTY   And off we went. He had a car.

DOPE KING (*Lighting a cigarette*)   Get in.

The Dope King takes out a black rag.

BETTY   What's that black rag?

DOPE KING (*Blindfolding her*)   I'm going to have to blindfold
you girls seeing as how I am the Dope King of Providence,
Rhode Island.

BETTY   Ooooo, I love an expert. Shut up, Betty. Just shut up.

DOPE KING   Lookit, you little twats, if you ever got caught,
you couldn't reveal where I'd taken you. You couldn't

betray me, but then I couldn't have you betray yourselves with the knowledge you knew where the dope headquarters of Providence, Rhode Island, was. I'm doing this for you, you little twats.

BETTY We drove, the three of us, my girlfriend, him, me. We giggled suicidally because maybe this man steering his car right then left then left then right would murder us and if he did we should remember where he took us. I had heard that directions given before death stay embroidered on your brain and the police can use that for a clue. I didn't care if we were murdered. My life was beginning. There was a hit song that summer. We drove singing it. (*She sings in a clear strong voice.*)

> Hey stay a while
> In the crook of my arms
> All you got to do is
> Look in my arms
> And you'll see Home Sweet . . .

Mavis, because that was my girlfriend's name, Mavis Brennan is squeezing my hand and I'm squeezing hers. Where are we? I smell bread. That Portuguese bakery. I think I know where we are.

DOPE KING We're here.

BETTY He led us out of the car. We held hands like mountain climbers. Doors open, stairs climb.

DOPE KING Okay.

BETTY Three steps. One. Two. Three. Doors shut.

DOPE KING Open your eyes.

Betty takes off the blindfold.

45

BETTY It was the room I had lived in the year before when I was working in the shoe factory for the summer. I saw traces on the wall where I had written "Fuck You" in peanut butter the year before one night because I was seventeen and my life still hadn't begun and I'm out supporting myself. I said, "Is Miss Carter still the landlady here? Is that the shoe factory over there?" I said, "Boy, some dope king. Living in a seventeen–dollar–a–week rooming house with breakfast thrown in on Saturday."

DOPE KING Some breakfast.

The Dope King goes.

BETTY We laughed and laughed.

BERT That's nice. You go to a strange place and they take off your blindfolders and it's a place where you lived.

BETTY That is precisely what I did not, underline the *not,* did not like. I remember Miss Carter had said, "What's that word in peanut butter on the wall?" I said, "Oh, you think that says *Fuck*? You dirty lady. That's a message in speed writing: If You See Kay. Kay was my girlfriend," I said. "If you see Kay, remind us both to rd ths msj and gt a bttr jb." Memories within memories. I'm remembering what I remembered in my memory . . .

BERT Where's Mavis?

BETTY She died or something.

BERT Mavis Brennan.

BETTY Don't be such a busybody.

BERT Mavis Brennan.

BETTY   What am I telling you stories about dope for? I should be telling you stories about how I didn't take dope. I should be a father influence to you.

BERT   How did you die?

BETTY   Who died?

BERT   Mavis Brennan.

BETTY   Don't be so morbid. I didn't say she died.

BERT   You said she died.

BETTY   Or something.

BERT   What's the something?

BETTY   You lose touch. Touch gets lost.

BERT   Will I lose touch with you?

BETTY   You're my kid. You're me. You're the fruit of my loins or the fruit of my loom. Some jokes Mavis and I used to make about phrases in the Bible. Jesus came riding into town on his ass. We'd laugh. I wish sometimes you were a girl. I wish sometimes I had a friend. Mavis Brennan.

BERT   You can call me Mavis.

BETTY   Mavis, I'm in love with a boy named Bert.

BERT   Do you love him a lot?

BETTY   More than life itself.

BERT   Do you love life?

BETTY   More than Bert himself.

BERT   Do you love me?

BETTY   But Mavis, you're my best friend.

BERT   Can I rub your hair?

BETTY   Oh, yes, Mavis.

BERT   (*Rubs her hair*)   When I rub your hair, I can feel the oil from it under my fingernails. I sit in class and the teacher says, "Get your fingers out of your nose." He says, "You can always tell the Catholic kids from the Protestant kids." He says, "The Catholic kids are always picking their nose and the Protestant kids are always biting their nails." He's bald and he says, "Grass doesn't grow on busy streets."

BETTY   You tell him grass doesn't grow on rocks either. This feels so good . . . don't stop . . . Bert . . . Mavis . . .

BERT   (*Goes to sink, gets a tray containing basin, pitcher, water, and shampoo*)   I'm getting the basin.

BETTY   I washed my hair last night.

BERT   Let me wash it tonight? Please? Momma, we have a thousand dollar bills in consecutive numbers. You are loved. You have decisions to make. Momma, let me clear your head. You always think better when I wash your hair.

He pours water over her hair. She leans back. Her hair is undone. Bert soaps it.

BETTY   Make it lather up. Push all the thoughts, the bad thoughts, push them out of my head.

BERT   Push 'em out. Push 'em out.

BETTY   (*Loving the shampoo*)   Wasn't he disgusting?

BERT   That man?

BETTY   (*Looking at the flowers he brought*)   Durwood Peach.

48

BERT   If you married him, you'd be Betty Peach.

BETTY   I'll give him back his money tomorrow.

BERT   Here comes the hot water!

BETTY   I'll keep half the money. A consideration fee. For considering his proposal.

BERT   Keep all of it. I don't want him around.

BETTY   No, I'll keep half the money in payment for a tormented night's sleep. For tossing and turning and wondering whether or not I should run away with an insane Good Humor Man. Ex–Good Humor Man.

BERT   Our flavor of the week: Betty Peach! Betty Peach on a stick! Here comes the shampoo. Make the bubbles come up. Work out all the bad thoughts.

BETTY   I went to visit Mavis in Memorial Hospital. She was dying of everything. They had cut off her breasts and she had lots of radiation treatment and her hair had gone. And I came to visit her. She was down to about sixty pounds and she wouldn't die. And I said, "Mavis, is there anything I can do for you?" And she said, "Yes, there is this new book, *The Sensuous Woman*. Bring it. Read it to me." And I went all that summer in Boston. Every day for visiting hours and read her from this dirty book on how to be sensuous and how to be attractive and how to have orgasms and how to . . . All summer she wouldn't die. All summer I read to her. I finished the book. Mavis said, "Begin it again." And I'd have to get very close to her to read because it was on the ward and the other patients did not want to hear this dirty stuff. And her gums were black and her breath smelled like sulfur and her hair was gone and I'm reading to her how to attract a man and she's smiling and hanging on. I never went back after one day. I couldn't go back. Fall was coming. I hated life. I hated Mavis. I hated. Rub the hair. Wash it out. More hot water. More bubbles. More soap. Get it all out of my head all the bad into a bubble and fly it away and pop it. Get it out.

Betty has torn all the petals off Durwood's flowers.

BERT (*Very moved, very tender*) The next time my biology teacher rubs his bald head and says "grass doesn't grow on busy streets," I'll say, "Yeah, and it doesn't grow on rocks either." I'll say that. I kiss your hair, Momma.

BETTY And I kiss Mavis and you and Raulito and your father and the Dope King of Providence, Rhode Island, and my sister Rosalie and life for bringing us a thousand dollars through the door and I kiss life and I kiss all the people I ever loved . . .

BERT Me! Me! Most of all me!

Bert pours water over her hair. The soap is washed out. Durwood appears in the room. He is breathless and excited.

DURWOOD Is something wrong with me? I have you here and say good night like some goon. What am I being so polite about? I'm no goon. Good manners make you a goon. I'm trying to learn to listen to myself. Listen to what I want. Not what people tell me I should want. You must think I'm a goon. Only a goon would drive thousands of miles to find the only woman he ever loved, find her, then leave her and go back alone to a room in the Dixie Hotel by himself.

BETTY What did I do to make you feel all this?

DURWOOD I remember riding by your house looking up at the porch, ringing the bells extra loud so you'd come down and buy ice cream from me. Your mother was sitting there rocking and your father reading a paper and you and your sister crouching on the green steps holding your skirts down around your ankles talking so hard to each other.

BETTY They're all gone mostly.

BERT You're gonna catch a cold. You got to dry the hair or the wet picks up dirt. Ma?

DURWOOD You and your sister walked down the steps still talking so hard you didn't even pay any attention to me and you bought vanilla and walked back up the stairs and sat down and kept on talking.

BETTY What in God's name could we have been talking about?

DURWOOD I said I want in. One day I'm going to be on that porch with that girl.

BETTY Her leaving home? Some Ava Gardner movie?

DURWOOD I realize now I wanted the girl and not the porch. (*He takes out snapshots.*) You got to come back with me. This house will be yours. All this land.

BERT Look at all the fences. Everything is outlined.

DURWOOD (*Tearing up the photos*) But if I had to choose between where I live and you, I'd rip up everything I own because the only landscape worth looking at is the landscape of the human body. I kiss your Blue Ridge Mountains of Virginia. I kiss your Missouri and Monongahela and Susquehanna and Shenandoah and Rio Grande. I kiss the

confluence of all those rivers. I kiss your amber waves of
grain. I kiss your spacious skies, your rocket's red glare,
your land I love, your purple mountain'd majesty. But most
of all I kiss your head. I kiss the place where we make our
decisions. I kiss the place where we keep our resolves. The
place where we do our dreams. I kiss the place behind the
eyes where we store up secrets and knowledge to save us if
we're caught in a corridor on a dark, wintry evening. And
you, with your mouth, kiss my head because that's the place
where I kept the pictures of you all these years. Come
home with me to the hotel.

BETTY   I will come with you.

DURWOOD (*Takes her aside*)   But you can't take the kid.

BERT   What is he saying?

DURWOOD   I don't want you having any children except
what comes out of us.

BERT   What are you talking?

DURWOOD   A family is like a body. A perfect body. The
man's the head. The woman's the heart. The children are
the limbs. I don't want any limbs from any other bodies.
No transplants allowed. You hear me? Only out of us.

BERT   What are you saying?

BETTY (*Taking Bert aside*)   Let me go down there and
check out the landscape. I'll send for you in a few days.
I swear.

Rosalie appears.

ROSALIE   So they went to South Carolina. The two of them.
They left the boy home.

Holahan appears.

HOLAHAN   So she claims. So she claims. The fact remains the
  kid is dead.

Betty holds out the money. Bert takes it. Betty and Durwood leave.

Bert comes downstage and sings.

BERT   I used to believe
       When I was young
       I understood
       Every note that was sung.
       Voices of sparrows
       Voices of blue jays
       Voices of robins

       Voices of eagles.

       When I was young
       I used to pretend
       Through all of my life
       I'd have a friend
       We'd climb the mountains
       We'd cross the deserts
       We'd sail the oceans
       We'd solve the mysteries.

       When I was young
       I used to believe
       In some other life
       I was an Inca
       Maybe a druid
       More like Egyptian
       Pyramid builder
       Leader of millions.

I used to believe
When I was young
I understood
Every note that was sung . . .

Voices of eagles

CURTAIN

ACT TWO

The interrogation room at the police station.

HOLAHAN We had trouble tracking you down. You left town. Everybody thought you had taken the boy with you.

BETTY I went away for a few days. He's a big kid. He's supposed to be able to take care of himself. Boy Scouts go off. Survivor camps where they go off, kids, for three months, four, in mountains. Kids go in forests for weeks and months and they come out men and parents are applauded.

HOLAHAN Bleecker Street ain't exactly survival camp.

BETTY He was supposed to stay with people in the building, people were supposed to look after him.

HOLAHAN A fourteen-year-old kid? Where's your head, lady?

BETTY Here. This whole area above the neck. I didn't just desert him. I left him with money. I left him with a thousand dollars.

HOLAHAN You left your kid with a thousand dollars?

BETTY My friend that I traveled with gave it to him. To me. I gave it to Bert.

HOLAHAN Even with inflation, a thousand's a lot of money.

BETTY What I'm saying to you is find the person stole the thousand dollars, you'll find who murdered Bert. Said it. I said murdered Bert. I promised myself everything would be all right if I never mentioned the word *murdered*. If I just never said the word, I'd be all right. If I never said the word, the person who . . . *did* it—

HOLAHAN The murderer—

BETTY Would be found.

HOLAHAN Stop running away from the fact!

BETTY I am not running away from the fact—

HOLAHAN Of the murder—

BETTY I just promised myself I wouldn't name the fact. Not ever. You made me say the word.

HOLAHAN Can I make you say another word you're avoiding?

BETTY Confess? Mister, I can say the word *confess* all that I want because saying the word *confess* is like saying the word *desk. Chair. Necktie. Dirt. Room. You.* I have nothing to confess.

HOLAHAN Where is this millionaire now?

BETTY It was only a thousand.

HOLAHAN This thousand–aire. Where is he right now?

BETTY South Carolina.

HOLAHAN That's where you went?

BETTY Solomon Ferry. The Peach family. Durwood. His father's name. He was a junior.

Holahan dials the phone.

Rosalie appears. She drags a chair and sits in it.

ROSALIE Scene. In which Betty wishes her sister was still alive so she could tell her what happened.

Betty sits against Rosalie's knees.

BETTY We got down to South Carolina two days after what a night at the Dixie Hotel. Durwood wasn't kidding all right. We came down this alley of trees and he says, "Close your eyes and now turn 'em on." He had this farm with white fences. I never saw so many white fences. I'm not even talking about what went on inside the white fences. I'm a country girl. No stranger to the green. The horses and cattle. I never saw such fences. And roads. White-painted rocks lining the roads pointing the way where you go up to the big house. I said, "Boy, old girl, you hit pay dirt this time. Boy, old girl," I said, "you have been on adventures in your short lifetime, but this is the key adventure. They're going to be doing TV spinoffs and shooting sequels to this part of your life. You are going to be a southern lady." We stop in front of the white farmhouse and this youngish lady soon destined to be the ex-wife who wrote me the note struts out of the farmhouse followed by these two old people you just want to hug with a real nice parents' look followed by golden dogs the color gold of cough drops that rescue you in the middle of the night. Durwood gets out of the car and I let him walk around the car to let me out. And these people instead lead him in the house instead of letting him open my side of the door. The woman who would soon be Durwood's ex-wife came back out and said, "Are you the girl from Maine?" I said, "Yes, I am." She said, "You're very kind to bring Durwood back to us. Here's money." I got out of the car. I said, "I'm going to live here." The old people said, "Thank you for bringing our

57

boy back to us. Here's money. He had to get you out of his system. We let him go to you. The doctors said let him go. It was the only way." I said, "Hey, this is going to be my house." "Well, one thing Durwood isn't crazy about," they said, "is you. You sure are a pretty girl. He's been talking years about you. But it's time he goes back in for a rest. There's a bus leaving two-oh-five from Crossroads Corner going to Wheeling, West Virginia, direct and you can make connections there back to Maine." I said, "New York. I live in New York now." They said, "Isn't that nice." They gave me fifty dollars and showed me the hospital where Durwood would be which was very pretty too with a little pond in the front of it and the dog rode in the car with us and licked my face and I loved those old people and asked them to take me with them. And they said, "Here's your bus," and I got on it.

The two sisters hold each other's hands. Holahan returns.

HOLAHAN We called the Peach family, honey.

BETTY Don't call me honey. Okay?

HOLAHAN They told us you were there.

BETTY So I'm free. Alibis.

HOLAHAN Honey, you don't need alibis for South Carolina. You need alibis for Bleecker Street. That's the required address of your alibis, honey. You could've killed Bert before you left so you wouldn't miss out on a joy ride to southern climes. Your boy putting cramps deep in your lifestyle. The Peach family of Solomon Ferry don't tell me nothing. The main event we're conferring about took place in New York City.

Melodramatic music. The lights go out on Betty and Holahan.
Rosalie appears. She speaks urgently, like one of those action-news
reporters covering a live event.

ROSALIE   Scenes containing information the police would
never know. Scenes containing information the mother
would never know, never could know.

Bert and Donny appear. Bert is flashing some of Durwood's money.

BERT   Hey, Donny my man.

DONNY   Hey Mr. Bert my man.

BERT   Want to see what I got? Not so close.

DONNY   You want to sneak into Monosodium Glutamate?

BERT   What's your mouth talking, my man?

DONNY   M.S.G. That's what rock musicians call Madison
Square Garden. Monosodium Glutamate. You know the
stuff they put in Chinese restaurants that makes your face go
all measles? You want to sneak in there tonight?

BERT   To a Chinese restaurant?

DONNY   To Madison Square Garden. They got hockey or a
concert or a flower show.

BERT   My man, if I go to Monosodium Glutamate, I go
walking right in the front door paying my own way. (*He
takes out a bill.*)

DONNY   Where'd you get a ten? You pulling jobs yourself?
Hey, I'm the man with the monkey. You into money now
by yourself? You deal me in. I got the dibs on the monkey.

BERT   No jobs by myself.

DONNY   You dealing? Coke? Pills? Is that more bills in there? They counterfeit?

BERT   No, my man. They are real as a summer's day.

DONNY   Bullshit. Those are counterfeit. That's play money.

BERT   You want to see? We go into the bank.

A bank counter appears. The teller stands behind it.

ROSALIE   They go into the bank on Sheridan Square. They wait in line.

BERT   (*To the teller*)   My man, is this bill negotiable? What I'm saying is there's no doubt about the accuracy of this denominational piece of merchandise.

The teller takes the proffered bill and holds it up to the light.

DONNY   They got a sign in the A&P saying beware ten-dollar bills being circulated.

The teller smiles and hands the bill back.

BERT   It's real? There's no doubts? And if I had more with serial numbers right in line, they'd all be real too? Thank you, my man. Here's a quarter. A tip for your appraisal.

ROSALIE   They walk away from the bank clerk. The bank is crowded.

BERT   (*Bert goes to a glass desk in the bank.*)   Come here. I want to do something. It's a funny joke I saw about a bank. You take—anybody looking?— a deposit slip and you write on the back: Hand over all your money or I blow your brains on the wall.

DONNY   Where'd you get that money?

BERT   Then you put the deposit slip back where it came from.

DONNY   Come on. Tell.

BERT   Then you wait.

Raulito enters the bank. He takes a deposit slip, fills it out, goes to the teller, who takes the deposit slip. The teller looks around, panicky. He pushes a button. A siren. Gunshots. Raulito looks around, his chest covered with blood. Blood comes out of his mouth.

RAULITO   I come into the bank to make deposit number seventeen in the Christmas Club. Time to make deposit number seventeen. Christmas Club.

He falls. His trench coat opens. His blood-spattered evening gown tumbles down. He falls dead. Music. Darkness. Bert and Donny run out.

DONNY   Buy me something. Your money's burning holes in my pockets. Let's go.

ROSALIE   They go.

Joanne has joined Bert and Donny.

DONNY   Hey, Joanne, Bert's crazy. You know what he's doing? Putting razor blades in Frisbees and then when we see somebody we don't like from Elizabeth Irwin High School, we toss it at them and say, "Hey, grab!"

JOANNE   Papers, I read a German shepherd ate a newborn baby.

BERT   Shut up, Joanne.

DONNY   Bert's mother's been gone two days now. She left him a lot of money.

JOANNE The mother went out and left the baby for a moment and the dog ate the baby.

BERT Shut up, Joanne. You're a real creep. My mother's right. You're a walking exorcism picture. All the time you're so creepy.

JOANNE Your mother likes me.

BERT She says you give her the creeps.

DONNY Momma's boy.

BERT I'm not!

JOANNE You are so.

BERT I like my mother being away. I got the apartment to myself. I'm eating good. Boy, my mother's a rotten cook. I see those commercials: Food like mother used to make. I say, Boy, that's the worst commercial God ever made.

JOANNE Momma's boy.

BERT Shut up. There's the restaurant where the bicycle got my aunt.

DONNY What kind of bicycle?

BERT Ten-speed Raleigh. Yellow.

JOANNE You got the money. You could buy a ten-speed Raleigh yellow. If you weren't so chintzy.

BERT No way. Money's got to last me.

DONNY She was a nice lady.

BERT That's how we came down to New York from Maine. We had her funeral, then we stayed and stayed. Wasn't for that ten-speed Raleigh whizzing around the corner we'd still be in Maine.

JOANNE   Momma's boy.

DONNY   Where's your father? My mother says how come we never see Bert's father?

BERT   He's away on secret duty.

JOANNE   Oh sure.

BERT   He's on the payroll of foreign governments. He calls me all the time and asks me not to tell where he is because if it got out.

JOANNE   Oh sure.

DONNY   The CIA?

BERT   More secret than the CIA.

JOANNE   Nothing is more secret than the CIA.

BERT   If it's such a good secret then how come you know about the CIA? The place my father works for is so secret it don't have no name or initials or nothing.

JOANNE   Or existence.

Margie appears.

JOANNE   Hey, Margie? Want to sneak in to what's playing at the Greenwich? The Waverly? I don't care.

The two girls go.

BERT   What a creep.

DONNY   German shepherds are gonna eat her someday.

BERT Suppose one day your money runs out and you don't know anybody, what do you do?

DONNY You work.

BERT Fourteen you can't work. They put you in orphanages? You go to the police, they arrest you? What do you do?

DONNY You got all this money.

BERT Suppose it runs out.

DONNY Thousand dollars don't run out.

BERT Sure it can.

DONNY You sure you got it?

BERT You want to see it?

They run.

Bert's apartment.

BERT Hello?

DONNY You think there's anybody here?

BERT Ma?

DONNY Is she here?

BERT I hid the money behind the curtains. I hid the money in the toilet. I hid the money in the freezer. I hid the money under the bed. I hid the money in the oven. I hid the money under the carpet. I hid the money in the shower. I hid the money in our shoes. I hid the money in the pockets of the clothes we don't wear. I hid the money. (*His arms are filled with bills.*) How long can it last me? Suppose somebody

64

comes in the window. Suppose they steal the money? Who am I gonna call? It's not me. It's a friend. I'm talking about a friend. What if my friend gets locked out? How will he get back in? Is there an earthquake? Why is the room shaking? I can't stop shaking! Hold down the floor! I don't know where she is! She went away and left me! She went out the door! She left me! She went away! I'm turning to water! My stomach's coming up! The floor is moving! (*He grabs onto Donny.*)

DONNY   Hey. Don't you hug me. Hey. You don't touch me. You hear me? You get your mitts off me. You hear.

BERT   I'm going away. Hang on to me.

DONNY   You keep your hands to yourself. You keep your hands. It was your idea bringing those guys up here and hitting them. You the one that brought them up. You brought up too many. You got too many watches, Bert. You stay away from me.

BERT   Suppose she never comes back?

DONNY (*Takes out his monkey wrench*)   I know what this is. You brought me up here to get my watches, didn't you? You earned all that money. You brought me up here. You're doing recruiting for those old guys down at the docks who want kids.

BERT   Suppose she don't ever come back.

Bert clutches Donny around his knees. Donny lifts his monkey wrench over Bert's head. They freeze. Rosalie appears with Durwood and Raulito and the Dope King and any number of identified people behind her.

ROSALIE   And all the dead people, the people who have died, me, Raulito, Durwood, the Dope King of Providence, Mavis Brennan, the man on the ten-speed bike, all the dead people in our lives join together and lead Donny to the wrench and put his hands around the wrench and lead the wrench to Bert's head and we hold Bert's head so Donny can bring the wrench down onto Bert's head with greater ease. Bert falls.

Donny takes the thousand dollars.

ROSALIE   And at this time precisely, Betty was being put on a Greyhound bus at Crossroads Corner, South Carolina, and being sent back to New York. Betty turns around in the window and sees the parents of Durwood and Durwood's wife waving good-bye.

Rosalie and the dead people go.

Donny stands over Bert's body. Joanne knocks on the door. Donny looks up, terrified.

JOANNE   Bert? Donny?

DONNY   Go away.

JOANNE   You in there?

DONNY   Get out of here, Joanne.

JOANNE   I'm coming in.

DONNY   You stay outside there.

JOANNE   I just got a summer job.

DONNY   Don't come in.

JOANNE   Checkout girl at the A&P.

Joanne struggles to open the door. Donny holds it shut. Joanne pushes the door in. Donny falls back.

JOANNE   You got to be very strong to be a checkout girl at the A&P.

DONNY   You tell and I'll—

Joanne sees Bert and walks around his body.

JOANNE   That's what a dead person looks like?

DONNY   He made me do it.

JOANNE   All the time you read about dead people and hear about dead people but this is my first. Not embalmed or anything.

DONNY   He tried to touch me.

JOANNE   Just regular dead.

DONNY   He put his hands on me.

JOANNE   I'm glad it's Bert. I'd hate for my first dead person to be a stranger.

DONNY   I'm not ever going to not believe in dreams again. I dreamed the other night and the night before that and once about six months ago that a yellow Checker Cab stopped and a man got out and dragged me in and when the cab stopped we were in a quiet warehouse so you could look down and see the river and waiting in a line was all these men with drool coming out of their mouths and my feet were in cement and the old man touched me only he wasn't old anymore and that dream came true just now. Bert was the old man. My feet were in cement. I am not going to end up my life in any dream. I stopped that dream.

Anybody tells you dreams don't tell the future you send them to me.

JOANNE   We'll say somebody killed him.

DONNY   Who killed him?

JOANNE   One of those guys you bring up here with the watches.

DONNY   I don't want any part of it. Cops up here. They'll find fingerprints.

JOANNE   Okay. They've had all those murders down at the docks. We'll put Bert in a bag and bring him down the river and leave him there. By the warehouse.

DONNY   But those murders. The school-crossing lady told me those bodies—they had no heads. The maniac takes the heads off.

JOANNE   You got a saw?

DONNY   There's one out there.

JOANNE   You start cutting. Put papers down.

DONNY   Is this a crime!

JOANNE   He's already dead. You're making a mess.

DONNY   My uncle saw a dirty movie and he told me Bert's mother was in it.

They take Bert by the feet and drag him into the dark.

JOANNE   Bert wasn't from here. Bert never belonged here.

They are gone. Betty appears in the light, at a phone. She dials. Rosalie appears.

ROSALIE   Betty is now in Washington, D.C. She roams around Washington, D.C., looking at monuments. She buys a dress to calm herself. She calls Bert from a pay phone.

The phone rings. Donny and Joanne come into the room.

JOANNE   Don't get it.

DONNY   It might be for me.

JOANNE   Don't get it. I'll wait for you outside.

Donny and Joanne go.

ROSALIE   Betty hangs up. She walks to the Capitol building to look for the Declaration of Independence she saw printed on parchment paper like the original. She will bring it home to Bert for a present.

Betty goes. Donny and Joanne appear in the street. Joanne pushes a shopping cart.

DONNY   I'm finished. I put him in a duffel bag.

The two of them drag the bag containing Bert.

JOANNE   Here's a shopping cart.

DONNY   We can't steal that. The A&P arrests you.

JOANNE   I'm going to be working there this summer. Employees are allowed to use them.

They load Bert's body in the bag into the cart. They begin pushing.

DONNY   You can smell the river tonight.

Margie comes up.

MARGIE   Hi. Joanne, could I talk to you?

JOANNE   Go away, Margie.

MARGIE   I got to talk to you.

JOANNE   Later, Margie.

MARGIE   What's in there?

DONNY   Margie, I believe Joanne was talking to you.

MARGIE   I want to see what you are pushing.

JOANNE   My grandmother's dog died and we're going to bury it in the river.

MARGIE   Can I walk with you? I don't want to go home yet. My mother's watching television. My father's kicking ass in the living room.

The three of them walk.

MARGIE   I went to the Waverly. My girlfriend held open the exit door. They had this movie there. A French picture. Reading the bottom lines in English while they're all above talking French. This picture was all about children. And a little French baby in the picture falls out of the nine-story window and lands nine stories on the ground and all the grown-ups are scared shitless and the baby—God, I screamed—lands on a bush and jumps up and says, Baby fall boom boom. The audience cheered. And later on this French grown-up says, That's childhood. They're protected forever. In a magic circle. Bad things happen to grown-ups but children are magic. I think that's what it said. I had to read fast and I was crying. I don't ever want to grow up. I'm afraid of getting out of school. I hate what's happening to my body. It's like it's a sin. I keep going to confession and confessing that things are happening to my body and the priest says, But that's growing up, and I said, I don't want to grow up. I mean, I want to grow up so I can leave home and get a job and make some money and get a record

70

player and get married, but I want my body to stop doing what it's doing. What kind of dog was it?

DONNY I don't like it down here.

JOANNE Look at the yellow cabs. People are pulling up. Going into those warehouses. People climbing into those trucks.

DONNY It's like my dream.

The cart tips over. Bert's head rolls out. Margie screams. Donny puts it back in the bag. Joanne takes Margie's hands. She and Donny put Margie's hands in the bag. Maggie struggles. Her hands are bloddied.

JOANNE You're part of this forever and ever. You're part of it.

MARGIE I'm out taking a walk.

DONNY Here's money. Don't tell.

JOANNE Shut up, Donny.

MARGIE Where'd you get that money?

JOANNE Don't give it to her.

DONNY She'll tell.

JOANNE She won't.

MARGIE I got to go home!

JOANNE You are part of this.

MARGIE I never saw nothing. My brain is dead. You hear me? I swear. My eyes are blind. I was never out. My ears don't hear. My brain is dead. I'm just out taking a walk. My brain don't register nothing. My eyes don't see. Forever. I'm never seeing nothing. Please. I'll see you. Later. School. I'll see you tomorrow. That's all.

71

Maggie runs away. Donny and Joanne roll the bag back into the cart, then push the cart into the darkness.

There is a splash.

Rosalie steps forward. music plays "Hey, Stay a While," very bouncily, cheerily. Rosalie does the stripper's walk while talking to us.

ROSALIE So Betty returned to New York, called Raulito to make sure her job was still safe with Honeymoon Holidays and to make a wonderful joke about her southern adventure of the past few days and she smiled because she would make it sound funny like a wonderful guest on the Johnny Carson show. Some Cuban relative answered the phone and told her Raulito was dead, shot while trying to hold up the Chase Manhattan Bank. Betty laughed till she realized a truth was being told. She ran home and found the police waiting there and when they told her Bert was dead, her son was dead, for a moment she got Bert and Raulito mixed up in her head. They both couldn't be dead. She had this picture that her apartment had become a branch of Chase Manhattan and that's what Raulito was holding up. They took her down to the morgue and she asked why her son was on two tables. One large and one small. She identified his body. She identified his head. The room was identical to the one she had identified her sister in two years ago and somehow that comforted her, that she had been here before. She did not know, Betty, nor would she ever know that two drawers over from her son's was Raulito's body. Betty was taken into custody. Betty was questioned for a long time. Betty was released. (*The music stops.*) Months went by. A summer. Joanne and Donny were very nice to her for a while but kids get new friends and kids forget and Betty hardly ever saw Bert's friends anymore. She draws a circle on a map and sees an island thirty miles off the coast of Massachusetts is the farthest she can get away from New York, from the mainland, with the sixty-odd dollars she has in her account. She gives up the apartment. She takes the bus to Massachusetts. She steps onto the ferry. She looks at the houses of great families on the shore. She talks with a man of quintuplets born many years ago. Talk of family and children. The sea is autumn calm. Seagulls fly above.

Rosalie goes. We are on the deck of the boat as at the beginning. Holahan and Betty appear at the ship's railing.

HOLAHAN   You recognize me?

BETTY   Captain Marvin Holahan. Sixth Precinct Homicide.

HOLAHAN   (*Pulls off his disguise*)   What did you write in that note? A confession?

Betty throws sheets of small papers into the wind. They blow away.

BETTY   A confession. A full confession. I wrote down everything that happened. And it's all gone. There it goes. There's your case.

HOLAHAN   I got bounced. From the force. About six days after our meeting. I took a lot out on you. I was on probation at the time of our interrogation. I had a lot of secret pressures on me. I thought if I nailed you, they'd overlook this minor nothing drug bribe extortion rap they pinned on me which if the truth be known everybody on the force is involved with in one way or another. But they were looking for a patsy. I loved the way you stood up to me. I wanted you to be the killer. If I stayed with the force I would've found your boy's killer.

BETTY No matter. I got on the bus this morning and I started writing on little pieces of paper everything I ever knew. Everything that ever happened to me. Sentences. Places. People's names. Secrets. Things I wanted to be. I thought maybe out of all that I'd find the magic clue who killed my kid. I'd say I see.

HOLAHAN I tried to do investigations on my own to find the killer for a present to you. But you can't investigate outside the force. You need that power. You need . . . that secret power the force offers.

BETTY It bothered me at first not knowing who killed Bert. But then I thought of all the things we don't know. All the secrets in the world got put into a bottle and thrown in the sea and maybe someday I'll be walking along a beach and the bottle containing the message for me will wash up. If I don't know the answer, it's out there and one day maybe an incredible coincidence will occur and I'll know all I need to know. Or the murderer will come forward. Or I'll even forget once I had a secret. I'll remember I had a boy like I'll remember I once had a mother and once had a father and I'll try to keep piling the weight on to the present, so I'll stay alive and won't slide back. If I don't know, somebody knows. My life is a triumph of all the things I don't know. I don't have to know everything. I read Agatha Christies and throw them away when the detective says "And the murderer is . . ." The mystery's always greater than the solution. I was terrified to have a kid. I said before I got pregnant, I'll have a kid and the eyes will end up on one side of the face and all the fingers on one hand and all the toes on one foot and both ears on one side of the head. And Bert was born and he was perfect. And this is the only thing I know. There's got to be some order in there. I'm moving

74

to this new place and it has big houses with classical columns and maybe I'll find a job in one of them in a house owned by an old man who has an art collection and I'll read up on classical painters and maybe he'll ask me to marry him or maybe I'll kill him and get him to sign the collection over to me or maybe I'll love him and marry him. Or maybe I'll discover a secret inside me that will make the whole world better. I'm not discounting nothing. Maybe I'll be transplanted into somebody great who knows the secret, my secret, or maybe I'll never know and a tornado or a water spout will whisk me up and I'll turn into rain and end up in that sea.

HOLAHAN   All I know is I know more about you than anyone I know. All those months doing dossiers on you. All disconnected. All disjointed. Still I know more about you. We both have to begin again. Maybe together? I could reveal myself to you slowly. That was not me who interrogated you. That was my job talking. That was unseen pressures talking to you. That was saving my skin talking to you. I feel for you. All what you've been through. I feel for you. I read stories people falling in love who threw acid in each other's faces and they get out of prison and they still love each other. I read stories people try to kill each other and end up loving each other. Give me a chance? I got severance pay? I got enough to get us through a winter?

Betty looks at him. Rosalie appears. Music: "Voices of Eagles."

ROSALIE   Last scene. In which Betty remembers the conversation she and I had so many years ago, the intensity of it burned into the Good Humor Man's head. Betty has tried to remember since that day what Rosalie, what I had told her. She remembers. She and I sat on a summer

75

afternoon on the green porch steps. Our mother over there. Our father over there. We pulled our skirts over our legs.

Betty and Rosalie sit side by side as young girls.

ROSALIE Stop shaking. Don't let them see. (*To their parents*) It's nothing, Dad.

BETTY It's like my stomach's going to come up all the time.

ROSALIE You're all right.

BETTY How am I going to get through my life?

ROSALIE Would you let me explain? Our spirits—it's so simple—float around in space and it all makes sense when you realize the planet Earth has these fishing hooks on it. What we call gravity is fishing hooks and all the nice things in the world are baited on those hooks and our spirits floating up there all loose and aimless spy those baited hooks and we bite. And we are reeled down onto this planet and we spend the rest of our stay on this planet trying to free our mouths of that hook, fighting, fighting.

BETTY But what do you do?

ROSALIE You travel alone because other people are only there to remind you how much that hook hurts that we all bit down on. Wait for that one day we can bite free and get back out there in space where we belong, sail back over water, over skies, into space, the hook finally out of our mouths and we wander back out there in space spawning to other planets never to return hurrah to Earth and we'll look back and can't even see these lives here anymore. Only the taste of blood to remind us we ever existed. The Earth is small. We're gone. We're dead. We're safe.

BETTY But Momma says—

ROSALIE   Oh, Momma says. Momma says. When are you gonna think for yourself?

BETTY   How do you . . . How can *I* think for myself?

Rosalie has no answer. Bells ring.

BETTY   Vanilla? You want vanilla? We hear you, Durwood!

Rosalie watches as Betty runs toward the ice cream. Betty stops. She turns to Holahan. She considers him. They move toward each other.

CURTAIN